CHAPPEL

ROAN

CHAPPEL

ROAN

CHAPPEL

THE LIFE, STYLE AND MUSIC OF

CHAPPELL ROAN

THE LIFE, STYLE AND MUSIC OF

CHAPPELL ROAN

UNOFFICIAL AND UNAUTHORIZED

BY NICK LEVINE

CONTENTS

WELCOME

PINK PONY *club*

An Introduction

Chappell Roan's mainstream breakthrough is nothing short of spectacular.

When she performed at the prestigious Coachella music festival in April 2024, Chappell introduced herself by saying: 'I'm your favourite artist's favourite artist.' This was a witty riff on a meme featuring *RuPaul's Drag Race* star Sasha Colby, who had branded herself 'your favourite drag queen's favourite drag queen' because her profile had yet to catch up with her potential. But now, Chappell is no longer a hotly tipped cult figure. She's a bonafide supernova whose dazzling debut album, *The Rise and Fall of a Midwest Princess*, has become a global chart-topper. She's also one of the most fascinating and distinctive artists of her generation.

Chappell's music is audacious, exhilarating and inescapable. After she made her chart breakthrough in April 2024 with 'Good Luck, Babe!', a synth-pop gem that doesn't appear on her album, her *Midwest Princess* bops 'Hot to Go!', 'Red Wine Supernova' and 'Pink Pony Club' also became huge hits. Other Chappell bangers have permeated pop culture in surprising ways: 'Super Graphic Ultra Modern Girl' has spawned countless TikTok mash-ups, while presidential nominee Kamala Harris used 'Femininomenon' in a campaign video.

As Chappell's music touches fans from New Zealand to Ireland, where 'Good Luck, Babe!' was a number one hit, she has also won plaudits from her peers. While performing in Munich in August 2024, Adele described Chappell as 'spectacular' and 'absolutely amazing'. When Olivia Rodrigo duetted with Chappell at an LA show that summer, she called her 'one of the most singular, inspiring, powerful artists I've ever had the pleasure of meeting'. Pop legend Elton John praised Chappell on Instagram for making 'brilliant pop music that brings the world together at a much-needed time'. These days, Chappell probably is, quite literally, your favourite artist's favourite artist.

Chappell may look like an overnight success story but, actually, her career is more than a decade in the making. She signed her first record deal in May 2015 when she was 17 and still calling herself by her birth name, Kayleigh Rose. This book will explore how an ambitious young woman who grew up feeling 'really weird' in a strict Christian community transformed herself into a drag-influenced superstar and Gen Z queer icon. 'I'm here to give back all the energy that the queer community has given to me,' Chappell told me when I interviewed her for *NME* in 2024.

This book will also recount the obstacles Chappell has faced along the way. Before she blossomed into the dynamic main-pop girl we know and love, Chappell pursued a different musical direction as a purveyor of 'really dark, angsty pop that was pretty boring' – those are Chappell's words, by the way, not mine. I'll also dig into the dizzying mix of music and style influences that make Chappell such an eye-catching performer.

However, success hasn't always brought Chappell unalloyed joy. Since she became famous, she has had to grapple with the loss of her anonymity and heavy expectations from fans and the media. There have been some bumpy moments, but Chappell is a game-changing artist because she pushes back against the status quo. Having worked so hard to become the person and performer she is today, she has no intention of getting pushed around. As she tells us on 'Super Graphic Ultra Modern Girl': ['I'm] not overdramatic, I know what I want.'

So, the story of Chappell Roan is one of struggle and self-actualization, kaleidoscopic pop magic and life-affirming big queer energy. Welcome to the Pink Pony Club – a place like no other that you won't want to leave.

THE ORIGIN STORY

★ OF A ★

MIDWEST *Princess*

Early Life and the Making of Chappell Roan

Chappell Roan wasn't born. She was created by Kayleigh Rose Amstutz, a talented and imaginative young woman who grew up in a sleepy part of the American Midwest feeling deeply confused.

As Kayleigh approached adolescence, she found it increasingly difficult to reconcile her strict Christian upbringing with her growing interest in bold, provocative pop music. Kaleidoscopic hits by Kesha, Katy Perry and Nicki Minaj dazzled and baffled her in equal measure. 'I was raised on Christian rock, but I never identified with it,' she told *NME* in 2024, long after she had adopted the stage name Chappell Roan. 'I felt such a push and pull because I was so curious about pop music but couldn't identify why I related to it. It was [talking about] a lifestyle I did not live.'

Kayleigh's own lifestyle was safe, staid and stifling. She went to a conservative Christian church three times a week, absorbing the damaging message that to be gay is a sin, and spent school holidays learning bible verses at Christian summer camps. She told *NME* her younger self was 'very sheltered' and 'very prude', so music videos flaunting risqué imagery blew her mind. In an interview with the *Guardian*, she recalled watching Lady Gaga's 'Alejandro' for the first time at age 12 and thinking to herself: 'Oh my god, is this porn?' But where there is tension, there is often a spark, and the inner conflict Kayleigh experienced during her formative years was to fuel her later songwriting. In time, she poured her growing pains into Chappell Roan, the gloriously gaudy drag persona with which she became a global star. But to understand Chappell Roan fully, we first need to understand Kayleigh's early life.

Kayleigh was born (on 19 February 1998) and raised in Willard, Missouri, a city with a population (6,344, according to the 2020 census) that makes it feel like a small town. In interviews, Chappell has described Willard as a 'green' and 'peaceful' place dominated by farms and churches, where 'everyone opens doors to each other'. By all accounts, her family life was loving and comfortable: her mum is a vet whose practice is managed by Kayleigh's dad, a registered nurse who has worked in intensive care units. She is the eldest of four siblings – she has a younger sister named Kamryn and two younger brothers, Dawson and Drew – and grew up with pets including a dog and a guinea pig.

Kayleigh didn't grow up with pushy stage parents. 'We're just a very normal household,' Chappell told local newspaper the *Springfield News-Leader* in 2017, two years after she signed her first record deal. 'No one in my family is musical, none of my cousins, no one in my immediate family.' Still, one family member's taste in music is immortalized in her stage name, which she adopted in 2016. Chappell is the surname of her late grandfather, Dennis, who died of brain cancer that year. Roan is a reference to an old cowboy song he loved, 'The Strawberry Roan' – the story of a pinkish-red horse that is the 'worst bucker' on the range. 'I let him hear rough demos, and I told him I was going to be Chappell in his honour,' Chappell told the *Springfield News-Leader*. 'He was really supportive of me.'

Other family members may not share the liberal political views that Chappell now espouses. In September 2024, she confirmed that she was voting for the Democratic Party's nominee, Kamala Harris, in the upcoming presidential election, but her uncle Darin Chappell is a Republican politician who serves in the Missouri House of Representatives. In 2024, *Newsweek* reported that he co-sponsored a bill to prevent public funds being awarded to abortion facilities in the state. Chappell has never spoken publicly about her uncle, but it's worth noting that she supports reproductive freedom through her page on social justice website Propeller. In 2024, Chappell and Propeller launched a competition to offer one lucky fan a pair of VIP tickets to her gig in Boulder, Colorado, complete with flights, accommodation and a post-show meet-and-greet. To enter, fans simply had to register their support for Reproductive Freedom for All, a nonprofit that lobbies for access to abortion, birth control, paid parental leave and protections from pregnancy discrimination. Chappell was using her most precious commodity – her time – to further a cause she really believes in.

Like many young people who find comfort in performing, Kayleigh didn't feel she fitted in. 'I felt so out of place in my hometown,' she told *Rolling Stone* in 2022. 'I wish it was better. I wish I had better things to say. But mentally, I had a really tough time.' Moments of respite came when she visited Ritter Springs Park, a 245-acre green space outside of Willard, and the nearby amusement park Silver Dollar City. She also enjoyed seeing plays in Springfield, the nearest big city, and going for dessert at Andy's Frozen Custard. In an interview with the Visit Springfield website, Chappell said she 'adores' Fantastic Caverns, a local show cave that takes visitors underground on a jeep-driven tram. Perhaps the dark theatricality of this experience provided escapism when Kayleigh was trying to reconcile her Christian upbringing with the supposedly 'sinful' thoughts she was starting to harbour.

EMERSON
BAD SUNS

Chappell told the Associated Press that when she got her first tattoo – a 'tramp stamp' of the word 'princess' on her lower back – it was essentially a middle finger to her 'very conservative' upbringing, when it was drummed into her that 'modesty is hottest'.

You can hear Chappell chafing against this mentality on 'After Midnight', a slinky disco bop from her debut album, *The Rise and Fall of a Midwest Princess*. 'My mama said, "Nothing good happens when it's late and you're dancing alone,"' Chappell sings. 'She's in my head saying, "It's not attractive wearing that dress and red lipstick."' Through her drag-influenced image, Chappell has continued to rebel against this mentality in spectacular and splashy ways. There's nothing modest about strutting on stage dressed as the Statue of Liberty, as Chappell did at New York's Governors Ball music festival in June 2024. She isn't the sort of pop star who tries to present a relatable, girl-next-door image.

During her formative years in Willard, Kayleigh also felt different because she was starting to realize that she might not be straight. Chappell told the *Guardian* that she 'grew up thinking being gay was bad and a sin', which cast a heavy shadow and left her feeling painfully isolated. 'I think that a lot of [my] songs are from daydreams, and a lot of that daydreaming happened from Missouri, from this repressed state of not having a queer community growing up and feeling really weird,' she told the Associated Press. 'Naked in Manhattan', a poignant synth-pop song from *The Rise and Fall of a Midwest Princess*, offers an evocative account of Chappell's first time with a girl as it's about to happen. When she sings 'could go to hell but we'll probably be fine', she is pushing any notions of sinful behaviour to the back of her mind. But in reality, Chappell wrote this song before she had ever been intimate with a woman. 'I was just yearning and longing for this feeling, and it was so close I could taste it, but I hadn't experienced it yet,' she told *NME*.

Trying to reconcile her queerness – a source of great joy and liberation – with the staunch Christian teachings of her childhood is an ongoing process. In 2023, Chappell told *Vanity Fair* that her relationship with religion was 'evolving' and framed its lingering impact on her in a more positive way. 'I don't identify with the Christian Church anymore right now, but I'm really glad that I was part of that community because I understand them,' she said. 'I understand that perspective. I know where they're coming from.'

I ♥ NY

Chappell also acknowledged, in a 2023 interview with *NME*, that 'it's really hard to rid yourself of internalized homophobia.' This kind of candour makes her a beacon of hope to young LGBTQIA+ fans who, like Chappell, are discovering that coming out is a journey rather than a destination. She certainly takes her responsibility as a queer icon and role model seriously.

*'I'm here to **give back** all the **energy** that the **queer community** has given to me,'*

she told *NME*. When Chappell appeared on 'A Carpool Karaoke Christmas' in December 2024, joined by her parents Kara and Dwight, she spoke movingly about her changing relationship with Christianity. 'I know for a lot of people, it's actually very freeing,' she said. 'For me it almost did the opposite, where I felt like I couldn't be myself, that who I was was a sin and I was going to hell no matter how good of a person I was or how much I loved God, for being gay. And I just couldn't handle feeling ashamed anymore.'

During her early teenage years, Kayleigh tried to keep a lid on these conflicting feelings. She has called her younger self a 'goody two-shoes' who 'wanted everyone to like me'. She balanced any furtive acts of rebellion with public displays of conformity. 'I snuck out a lot, but I still went to church three times a week, you know what I mean?' Chappell told *Variety*. 'So it was just this dichotomy of trying to be a good girl but also wanting to freaking light things on fire.' In the same interview, she described her childhood as 'really depressed', although no one at the time realized the extent of her mental health issues. Because she wasn't diagnosed as bipolar until she was 22, she had 'a difficult time' as a child because 'my parents just thought I was being a brat'. Now, in her late twenties, Chappell is still working hard to unpack and manage her mental health. She told the *Guardian* in September 2024 that a psychiatrist had recently diagnosed her with 'severe depression', something Chappell attributed to the way her 'whole life has changed' since she became globally famous.

While she was still trying to act like the archetypal Christian good girl, Kayleigh dreamed of a more exciting life as a performer. She was particularly drawn to the glitz and glamour of Hollywood award shows. 'Originally, I thought I was gonna be an actress and singing could be a way for me to get a foot in the door. I wasn't, like, a savant at music or anything,' Chappell told *NME*. She started teaching herself to play the piano at 'ten or eleven' and began formal lessons at twelve. 'I refused to learn theory because it was boring and I learned by ear and copying my piano teacher's hands,' she told *Illustrate* magazine. 'I also took vocal lessons for a couple years, but not classically. [My teacher] taught me how to really belt and sing with confidence. It was more of a pop approach to vocal lessons.'

A year later, when she was 13, Kayleigh performed in public for the first time. On the official Chappell Roan Facebook page, you can still find footage from her live debut, in which she sings 'The Christmas Song (Chestnuts Roasting on an Open Fire)' in her middle school gymnasium. Her voice has a youthful innocence, but she already sounds like the Chappell Roan who would go on to conquer the charts 13 years later with 'Good Luck, Babe!'. At 14, Kayleigh auditioned for *The Voice* and *America's Got Talent* but didn't make it onto either show. She later admitted she had 'no idea' what she was doing. Around this time, she started writing her own songs with Rihanna's mournful piano ballad 'Stay' as a frame of reference. 'I couldn't believe that so much emotion was in such a simple song,' Chappell told Refinery29. She also got into hip-hop music, especially the sad-boy laments of Canadian singer-rapper Drake. 'It was just a brand new world that I had not been exposed to ever. Hip-hop made me feel really cool and was a place where I could put all these angsty feelings,' she told *Variety*. Music was beginning to expand the seemingly parochial worldview that Kayleigh had grown up with.

Kayleigh polished her songwriting skills when she attended a summer camp at Interlochen Center for the Arts in Green Lake Township, Michigan. 'The teachers were like: "Here's some techniques you can use, here's some books you should read." And that was really helpful,' Chappell told *NME*. Her time at Interlochen also proved eye-opening on a personal level. 'It changed my trajectory forever,' she recalled in an interview with *Pride Source*.

'I'd never been with other songwriters before in my life that were my age. Everyone was a fucking hippie, and I'm from ***Trump country.*** *I'm from a heavily church background, and this is not that. There were kids from all over the world there.* ***It was just so inspiring.'***

At 15, she adopted the stage name Kayleigh Rose and began gigging in the Willard area. Some of her earliest shows took place in late 2013 at Cider Days, an arts and crafts festival in nearby Springfield, and a local coffee shop called The Bean in Bolivar. One Facebook fan who heard about Kayleigh Rose through the young singer's grandfather, Dennis Chappell, noted approvingly that she was a 'very talented, motivated young lady' who already had a 'great support team'.

During a set at Cider Days, Kayleigh Rose debuted 'Die Young', a striking original song she had written at Interlochen. Its anguished lyrics deal with the interconnected problems Kayleigh was dealing with at the time, including feeling rejected by her peers and disconnected from her parents. 'Look at your mama, now she's crying, 'cause she thinks her baby's dying,' she sings on the verses. Several years later, after she had released 'Die Young' as Chappell Roan, she wrote on lyrics website Genius: 'This whole song is about me not understanding how to deal with being depressed, and thinking no one else understands, but in reality, I had so many people there who loved me and were willing to help.'

Though 'Die Young' is far darker than the songs Chappell would eventually become known for, it definitely showed off her burgeoning musical talent. Interlochen songwriting teacher Seth Bernard told *Pride Source* in 2023 that Kayleigh had 'knocked me out' with 'Die Young' in particular. 'It's a really great, powerful song and I noticed that she was writing from a very mature place,' he said. After her Cider Days performance, she was approached by a local TV cameraman who wanted to branch out into music videos. He was so impressed with 'Die Young' that he offered to shoot a low-budget promo clip for free. 'So we went up to my garage with my mom, built this mini set and he filmed it, and that's what got me signed,' Chappell told Visit Springfield.

Kayleigh signed to Atlantic Records, an American label with superstars including Ed Sheeran and Bruno Mars on its books, in May 2015. By this point, she had already pressed pause on her formal education so she could focus on music, which she now regarded as her 'job'. She even begged her principal at Willard High School to let her graduate a year early, a request he granted. 'I was flying once a month to New York or LA because I was showcasing my music to record execs,' she told Visit Springfield. 'I was 16, I didn't know what was going on. I was doing math homework at the hotels and stuff. I was like, I literally can't do this, I'm going to break down.' To make sure she had enough credits to graduate, she took online classes at Brigham Young University, a private school based in Provo, Utah. It sounds like a bit of a scramble, but she got her diploma.

Kayleigh was clearly gifted and hyper-ambitious, but she didn't realize at the time quite how much she was sacrificing.

*'I didn't do my **senior year**, I didn't go to **prom**, I didn't go to **graduation**. I missed a lot of what would have been the end of my childhood to do this job,'*

she told *Rolling Stone* in 2022. In a subsequent interview with *Vanity Fair,* she revealed that she still mourns her childhood because 'My career took that away from me pretty immediately when I signed.' Still, a year after she joined Atlantic, she adopted a new stage name, Chappell Roan, and never looked back. Speaking to the Oxford University newspaper *Cherwell*, she described her pop star moniker as 'very sentimental' because of its connections to her grandfather. She also said, interestingly, that she had 'never felt super connected' to her birth name and still wished that her 'name was not Kayleigh in real life'. Chappell Roan was a bright, bold, brand-new persona through which she could explore previously hidden aspects of herself.

The rise of a Midwest princess had begun, but there were some serious bumps in the road ahead. Although Willard had felt suffocating during her teenage years, Chappell soon discovered that absence can make the heart grow fonder. On 'California', a reflective ballad from her debut album, she sings about the way she 'stretched myself across four states' to build a career. 'I miss the seasons in Missouri, my dying town,' she sings yearningly. In 2021, Chappell would return to Willard in less-than-ideal circumstances, but only after she completely recalibrated her musical direction. Chappell Roan didn't arrive fully formed; it took time for her to grow into a superstar.

A NOT-SO-CASUAL *Start*

Chappell's Early Career

m&m's
glaad
spirit day
m&m's
Kellogg's
spirit day
glaad
Kellogg's
m&m's
glaad
spirit day
m&m's
Kellogg's
spirit day

In August 2017, a little over two years after signing her record deal, Chappell was ready to release her first single.

She was only 19 and still living at home in Willard, but 'Good Hurt' was no tentative debut. The song and music video weren't just dropped online, but received a prestigious 'premiere' on *Interview* magazine's website. Positioning is pivotal when launching a new artist, and Chappell's label had chosen to align her with the iconic pop culture title co-founded by the great Andy Warhol. To borrow an expression-turned-meme from Mariah Carey: not everybody has that.

'Good Hurt' was a striking and sophisticated debut. Directed by Griffin Stoddard, who went on to work with Chappell again on 'Pink Pony Club', the video introduces us to a sombre and contemplative singer-songwriter. We see Chappell with acupuncture needles in her face, lying on broken glass and sitting in a bathtub at the bottom of an empty swimming pool. Her makeup is flawless but relatively plain and her long, flowing hair uncoloured. Nothing about this iteration of Chappell Roan is giving drag queen.

These vaguely gothic visuals suit the song, which is a soulful ballad that Chappell delivers in a deeper voice than she uses on her more recent hits. 'No one else compares to who I had first, all I really want is that good hurt,' she sings yearningly. In an annotation on lyrics website Genius, Chappell revealed that she wrote 'Good Hurt' in her hometown with Jennifer Decilveo, an award-winning producer who has since worked with Miley Cyrus and Demi Lovato. 'At the time, I was dating a really boring guy and there wasn't much going on in our relationship, unlike my previous relationship,' Chappell added. 'I wanted that toxicity and the pain my previous relationship brought me, because that's all I knew. It was very unhealthy.'

A LANDMARK RELEASE

Chappell's debut EP, *School Nights*, followed in September of that year. It opens with 'Die Young', 'Good Hurt' and the dramatic piano ballad 'Meantime', which Chappell singled out as the 'hardest' of the five songs to write. 'I was in this relationship and I felt like I couldn't give everything to them. So I was basically saying, "Can I love you in the meantime while I figure myself out?"' she told *Unclear Magazine*. Then comes 'Sugar Rush', the EP's most hopeful moment, on which she swoons over a 'candy man' whose 'cotton candy voice melts in my mouth'. The EP's fifth and final track, 'Bad for You', is more suggestive: 'Bet I know exactly what you're doing when you're alone in your room,' Chappell sings. 'Darling, tell me if you're having trouble and I'm sure I could help you.'

As a body of work, 'School Nights' lacks the playful spark of Chappell's later music, but it's accomplished stuff. 'Sonically, I'd say that it's very dark pop with some influences of the sixties and seventies,' she told AXS at the time. In the same interview, Chappell offered an insight into her songwriting process, which tended to begin with a 'feeling' as opposed to a concrete idea: 'I'll think of a melody and plug the lyrics in once I figure out what the song's about,' she explained. 'I also have a list on my phone filled with words and phrases that I hear people say, or with sentences from books that I think might be cool for a song.'

'School Nights' didn't trouble the charts, but Chappell supported its release by opening for Australian singer-songwriter Vance Joy on his autumn 2017 tour of North America. In her interview with *Unclear Magazine*, Chappell described life on the road as a 'whirlwind' and said the headliner's fanbase had been very 'open' and 'accepting' of her music. 'After my shows I go out and sign posters for people and that's my favourite part,' she added. She also expressed an intention to head to LA after the tour to finish her album. 'It was so different from home, where I always had such a hard time being myself and felt like I'd be judged for being different or being creative. I just felt overwhelmed with complete love and acceptance, and from then on I started writing songs as the real me.'

A MAJOR MOVE

In fact, Chappell relocated to LA for good in 2018, a move that had a seismic effect on her life and musical direction. On one of her first nights in the city, she walked into The Abbey, a legendary multi-room queer venue where go-go dancers knock shoulders with drag queens. Chappell was rapt. 'All of a sudden I realized I could truly be any way I wanted to be, and no one would bat an eye,' she told *Headliner* magazine. 'It was so different from home, where I always had such a hard time being myself and felt like I'd be judged for being different or being creative. I just felt overwhelmed with complete love and acceptance, and from then on I started writing songs as the real me.' In time, Chappell would channel her revelatory gay night out into 'Pink Pony Club', the song that completely rerouted her career.

But before then, she continued to pursue her dark-pop direction with a couple of standalone singles. Released in February 2018, 'Bitter' has a hint of country in its delicate, guitar-led production, but the lyrics are filled with mental anguish. 'Oh god, tell me that I'm not insane with a toy gun hanging in my mouth,' Chappell sings at the start. 'School Nights', which followed in March, was presumably intended for Chappell's EP of the same name – it's definitely strong enough to have made the cut. Chappell told *Anchr* magazine that this atmospheric mid-tempo track is about 'being in love for the first time' and 'being young and staying up late on a school night'. But in another interview from this period, she hinted that her songwriting was already evolving away from teenage angst. 'When I first started out, I was writing five-minute ballads, really slow and really long, but now I like writing songs that are catchier,' she told *The Daily Orange*.

The release of 'Bitter' and 'School Nights' coincided with another profile-boosting support slot. Between January and March 2018, Chappell opened for British singer-songwriter Declan McKenna on the North American leg of his *What Do You Think About the Car?* Tour, an experience she described as 'amazing'. This would be her last significant live engagement for some time because for the next two years, Chappell hunkered down and focused on songwriting. At the tail end of 2018, she met Dan Nigro, a former indie musician who had reinvented himself as a pop producer with credits on Carly Rae Jepsen, Kylie Minogue and Sky Ferreira albums. He quickly became Chappell's closest collaborator.

Their very first session together yielded 'Love Me Anyway', a shimmering dream-pop song that later became a single. Nigro told *Music Week* that after a 'slow' start, he and Chappell found their creative sweet spot. He played a drum loop and some guitar chords, then Chappell spent an hour concocting the first verse and chorus of 'Love Me Anyway'. 'I was blown away,' Nigro stated.

*'I thought, "Shit, what a **beautiful voice**, this person is **incredibly talented**." And from there, it all just **blossomed**.'*

A MUSICAL BREAKTHROUGH

Around five months after writing 'Love Me Anyway', Chappell walked into Nigro's studio and told him she wanted to write a dance song called 'Pink Pony Club'. In an interview with NPR, Nigro admitted he was initially nonplussed because her music had always been 'really dark and moody' in the past. But when he played a drum beat and they crafted the song's intro together, everything started to make sense. Inspired by her night at The Abbey, Chappell imagined the journey of a young woman from Tennessee who comes to LA to dance at 'a place where boys and girls can all be queens every single day'. It wasn't strictly autobiographical, but there are clear parallels with her own move from sleepy Willard to liberal Los Angeles.

At first, neither of the song's writers was convinced the song was a winner. 'I was embarrassed by it because I was like, "This is so cheesy!" And at that point, I was confusing cheesy and campy,' Chappell recalled in a 2023 *Variety* interview. Nigro felt even more conflicted. 'I've got this feeling a couple of times in my career of when you write a song that's so bold, your body starts to give you these weird mixed signals,' he told NPR. 'Because you start to like it so much and then you actually feel like it's special, but then you're afraid. You feel like, "Oh, are people going to understand this?"' Sadly, his instincts proved spot on. Because 'Pink Pony Club' was so different from her previous releases, Atlantic Records refused to release it. 'I literally delivered it to the label and they were like, "No." They said no for a year, and I believed them. I felt so defeated,' Chappell told *Variety*.

But Chappell stuck to her guns and eventually her label relented. She released 'Pink Pony Club' in April 2020, accompanied by a glittery video featuring drag performers Meatball and Porkchop. It was followed in May by two more singles, the dreamy 'Love Me Anyway' and 'California', a melancholy ballad about yearning for home. These would be Chappell's final releases as an Atlantic Records artist because two months later, she was dropped. 'I had a very small fan base, but they were scared I would lose it,' Chappell told *NME*. 'It was a hard left turn from my original EP, which was really dark, angsty pop that was pretty boring.' That's a somewhat harsh assessment of her *School Nights* era, but 'Pink Pony Club' definitely suggested a new way forward. It was almost like someone had flicked the switch from black and white to dazzling Technicolor.

A DEVASTATING MOMENT

Chappell took the news hard – 'I burst into tears,' she told *Rolling Stone* – and still remembers feeling completely cut adrift. When she won a Grammy for Best New Artist in February 2025, she used her acceptance speech to 'demand' better terms for developing artists. Her asks? A liveable wage and basic healthcare. 'When I got dropped, I had zero job experience under my belt, and like most people, I had a difficult time finding a job in the pandemic and could not afford health insurance,' she told her peers in the room and a TV audience of millions. 'It was so devastating to feel so committed to my art and feel so betrayed by the system.'

When she was dropped in August 2020, Chappell was also dealing with the breakdown of a four-year relationship with a male partner, which happened in the very same week. With no income stream and little to keep her in LA, it made sense for Chappell to move back to Missouri, where she worked in a drive-through coffee kiosk that took an innovative approach to iced beverages. 'It's the classic Midwestern thing where it's like, "We can make any candy bar you want into a frappé!" It was not my favourite,' Chappell recalled drily in an interview with *Variety*.

Chappell with her producer, Dan Nigro, at the 2024 ASCAP Pop Music Awards. Nigro and Olivia Rodrigo, whose music he also produces, were named Songwriters of the Year.

Chappell was never going to rebuild her career from Willard, so in October she returned to LA, where she worked as a nanny, at a doughnut shop and as a production assistant on an HBO show. But her music career was stuck, a problem compounded by the fact that Dan Nigro's was majorly taking off. In January 2021, Olivia Rodrigo released 'Drivers Licence', an affecting bedroom pop ballad produced by Nigro. It was an instant smash that broke streaming records and reached number one in 25 countries. Rodrigo's Nigro-produced debut, *Sour*, followed in May and became the fourth best-selling album of 2021 globally. Chappell's producer was suddenly a very big deal. 'That was his biggest year ever and I didn't want to get in the way of that,' Chappell told *Rolling Stone*.

AN ORGANIC TRANSFORMATION

Despite his rising profile and other commitments, it was Nigro who gave Chappell the pep talk she needed – and he didn't sugarcoat it. 'Dan was just looking at me and goes: "You are going to run your career into the fucking ground if you don't start doing shit on your own,"' Chappell told *Rolling Stone*. She didn't need to be told twice. Ever the grafter, Chappell reinvented herself as a 'thrift-store pop star' who used creative ways to circumvent her lack of major label money. She learned to do her own drag-inspired makeup, taught herself to embellish stage outfits and tapped friends for a freebie when it was time for a photoshoot. Though Chappell's no-frills approach arose out of necessity, it was also the making of her. Her new image reflected her burgeoning queerness and matched her emerging musical direction: she was now a bold, colourful pop star making bold, colourful pop music. In August 2021, culture website Vulture anointed 'Pink Pony Club', a single released 15 months earlier, the 'song of the summer'. Chappell's banger wasn't a mainstream hit yet, but it was picking up traction.

In February 2022, Chappell maintained her forward momentum by releasing her first single as an independent artist, the twinkly disco pop 'Naked in Manhattan'. By this point, she had signed a new publishing deal with Sony, but she was still a proud 'thrift-store pop star'. The song's deliberately grainy video shows her exploring New York City, seemingly on the hoof. 'Naked in Manhattan' was also a musical milestone because, for the first time, Chappell sang about her queerness in an overt way: 'Boys suck, and girls I've never tried, and we both know we're getting drunk tonight,' she sings with a glint in her eye. Ahead of its release, Chappell told journalist Bonnie Orbison that she wrote 'Naked in Manhattan' about her first 'girl crush'. As well as capturing the thrill of anticipation, Chappell's lyrics show off her flair for pop culture references. 'Let's make it cinematic like that one sex scene that's in *Mulholland Drive*,' she sings, alluding to a famous sapphic moment from the David Lynch movie.

A second independent single, the industrial synth-pop track 'My Kink Is Karma', followed in May. Chappell described it as an 'insanely toxic' breakup song, a fair summary given that it features the lyrics: 'My kink is watching you crashing your car, you breaking your heart.' That month, she capitalized on her growing buzz by opening for Olivia Rodrigo in San Francisco. Chappell's five-song set list concluded with 'Femininomenon', a giddy dance song that she released as a single later that summer. After a subdued piano and strings intro, 'Femininomenon' shifts gear massively to become a thumping female-empowerment anthem. Though it has one of Chappell's silliest hooks – 'Get it hot like Papa John!' – it's a song with a serious emotional core. On the verses, she sings about her unsatisfying relationships with men and looks ahead to an unhappy future 'stuck in the suburbs ... folding his laundry'. Chappell told Earmilk that when she wrote 'Feminomenon' – 'a queer anthem that had a sad undertone' – she was trying to be 'as ridiculous as I possibly can'. Chappell's swelling confidence as a songwriter also shone through on her next single, 'Casual', a regretful ballad about an ex who won't commit. By this point, any coyness in her lyrics had long since evaporated. 'Knee-deep in the passenger seat, and you're eating me out, is it casual now?' she sings with an implied eye roll. The music video illustrates the song's message with a romance between Chappell and an otherworldly sea siren played by actress Mika Leshā. Chappell wants them to move in together, but Leshā's siren will always return to the ocean. Chappell called it a 'gay version' of the mermaid movie *Aquamarine*.

A LIVE REAWAKENING

Chappell dropped 'Casual' at the end of October 2022, a few days before she began a ten-date engagement opening for pop singer Fletcher across the US. It was her first significant run of live shows since 2018, but she followed it pretty quickly with her first-ever concert tour as a headline act. When it began in February 2023, the 20-date Naked in North America Tour wasn't just an affirming moment for Chappell as an artist, but also an opportunity to underline her values. At each show, she booked local drag queens to warm up the crowd, an idea borrowed from queer country singer Orville Peck. 'It was so much the right thing to do – like, I think this every single night,' she told *NME*. 'I mean, it supports the local queer community and a lot of people have probably never seen drag as an opener, or even at all.'

After the tour wrapped in mid-March, Chappell released 'Kaleidoscope', a contemplative piano ballad about the complexities of queer love. It was her first single on Amusement Records, Dan Nigro's imprint of the major label Island. Chappell thought hard about ending her independent-artist era to join Island because she knew she could execute her musical vision without record company interference. She also had other label offers on the table. She told *NME*: 'I went in with the attitude [of]: "This is what I need – the only thing I need right now is money." I was very picky and I had a fuck ton of leverage.'

As if to prove her point, Chappell's next two singles were unapologetically queer pop bangers. In May she released the glorious guitar-driven 'Red Wine Supernova', which she described in a press release as 'a campy gay girl song that captured the magic of having feelings for another girl'. When Chappell deadpans: 'I heard you like magic – I've got a wand and a rabbit', it's a cheeky wink to two vibrating sex toys. Then, in August, she dropped 'Hot to Go!', an electro-pop headrush with cheerleader-style chants.

'It's like the Y.M.C.A. but ***gayer,'***

Chappell told Pop Crave. Filmed in Springfield, Missouri, the cute music video shows Chappell teaching the song's Y.M.C.A.-style dance moves to her grandparents and local drag performers.

Chappell had blossomed into the exciting, agenda-setting pop star she was always meant to be. More than six years after she dropped her debut single, 'Good Hurt', it was finally time to release an album. *The Rise and Fall of a Midwest Princess* was ready.

THE RISE & RISE OF A FEMININOMENON

A Story of 'Overnight' Success

"All the News That Fits"
VOTE! VOTE! VOTE!
ELECTION 2024
SPECIAL SECTION
Rolling Stone
Issue 1392
October 2024
A Star Is Born
CHAPPELL
ROAN

In September 2023, Chappell dropped her debut album, *The Rise and Fall of a Midwest Princess.*

It wasn't just a collection of songs; it was a glittering testament to her personal evolution. As she told *Rolling Stone* in release week, the project had helped her to 'come to accept' her queerness over time. 'When I started the album, I was in a four-and-a-half-year relationship with a man,' she explained. 'I was writing about girls and the thought of girls. I was like, "I'm going to write about the part that I always wanted to feel: just complete freedom and euphoria and sparkles." And I'm going to pretend like this is the only world that it lives in.' But now, this sense of queer euphoria wasn't imaginary; it was part of Chappell's everyday life, and she felt ready to be a role model. 'I feel like I represent the queer kid in the Midwest that broke out and just became a fucking dragon,' she said. 'The album is for the girl in high school who was like, "It's a phase. It's a phase. It's a phase." It's for my teenage self.'

By the time Chappell's album arrived, nine of its fourteen tracks had been released as singles, beginning with 'Pink Pony Club' more than three years earlier. Still, the five new songs gave fans plenty to process. Chappell described 'Super Graphic Ultra Modern Girl' as an 'undeniable gay pop song'. It's a powerful statement of intent set to a pounding house beat. The spoken word refrain – 'not overdramatic, I know what I want' – is her sassy way of clapping back against coded misogyny on the straight dating scene. 'I'm through with all these hyper mega bummer boys like you,' she sings on the chorus. The sleek neo-disco tune 'After Midnight' is affirming and transgressive. Over shuffling synths, Chappell tells us she's done with being a 'good girl' and wants to get 'freaky' with someone else's boyfriend (or girlfriend) under the club lights.

Chappell told *Rolling Stone* that 'Picture You', an undulating ballad inspired by a sexually charged online relationship, 'showcases my vocals in a way that no other song does on the record'. The lyrics are cleverly suggestive rather than overtly dirty: 'I'm too scared to say half of the things I do when I picture you,' Chappell sings teasingly. Meanwhile, 'Coffee' represents her vulnerable side – it's a song about wanting to reconnect with an ex platonically but knowing that temptation will get in the way: ''Cause if we do coffee, it's never just coffee,' Chappell sighs. The album's most experimental moment, 'Guilty Pleasure', comes right at the end. It begins as a pretty, stripped-down folk ballad before transforming into a giddy synth-banger complete with yodelling vocals. Chappell told *Rolling Stone* it represents the part of her musical that 'would love to go more weird and indie'.

CHAPPELL HITS EUROPE

The Rise and Fall of a Midwest Princess received glowing reviews from music critics, who labelled it 'uproarious', 'exuberant' and 'unabashedly fun', but it didn't chart in its week of release. From September through December, Chappell supported the album with the opening leg of The Midwest Princess Tour, which included her first-ever live shows in Australia and continental Europe. Fittingly, the leg concluded with two sold-out shows at Heaven, an iconic LGBTQIA+ venue in London that has hosted legends including Cher and Queen frontman Freddie Mercury. 'I felt honoured to be playing where Freddie Mercury used to party,' Chappell told *NME*. Inga Rock, a drag queen who opened for Chappell in London, described the atmosphere on both nights as 'electric' and extremely queer. 'When I asked the crowd: "Are there any bisexuals here tonight?", I almost got ear damage from the response,' Inga recalled. Chappell was finding her people all over the world, but at this point, she hadn't quite broken into the mainstream.

This all changed during the first half of 2024. In late February, Chappell began her five-week stint opening for Olivia Rodrigo on her *GUTS* World Tour. Playing to arenas packed with pop fans gave Chappell an instant boost: *Billboard* reported that streams of her catalogue rose 32 per cent in her first weekend on the tour. In March, she received another uplift when her Tiny Desk concert premiered and became a social media sensation. This long-running concert series hosted by NPR Music always benefits from the incongruous nature of watching musicians perform in a cramped, cluttered office, but Chappell doubled down on the dissonance. Rocking an enormous auburn wig and gloriously garish drag makeup, she performed five songs from her album accompanied by female musicians dressed in hot pink. The effect was weird, wonderful and campy in a quintessentially Chappell way. Various clips went viral on TikTok, many with comments praising Chappell's 'iconic' look and attitude.

Chappell and Olivia Rodrigo perform 'Hot to Go!' at Intuit Dome in Inglewood, California, in August 2024. Earlier in the year, Chappell had opened for Olivia on her GUTS World Tour.

CHAPPELL CLIMBS THE CHARTS

At the start of April, Chappell wrapped her run with Olivia Rodrigo, began the next leg of The Midwest Princess Tour and released 'Good Luck, Babe!', a brand-new standalone single. Co-written with Dan Nigro and Justin Tranter, an in-demand songwriter who has worked with everyone from Lady Gaga to Britney Spears, it was her most polished pop offering yet. Chappell told *Rolling Stone* that she set out to 'write a big anthemic pop song' and admitted it was 'a bitch' to get right. Happily, her hard graft paid off when 'Good Luck, Babe!' became her first charting single in most major territories. In its week of release, it debuted at number 77 on the US Billboard Hot 100 and number 64 on the UK's Official Singles Chart – a solid springboard for its future success. Chappell's touring momentum had brought her to the brink of a mainstream breakthrough, but 'Good Luck, Babe!' pushed her over the edge. It was the right song at the right time.

Later in April, Chappell capitalized on her growing buzz with a pair of incendiary sets at Coachella music festival in California. At the start, she introduced herself to the cameras by saying: 'My name is Chappell Roan. I'm your favourite artist's favourite artist.' She wasn't boasting about her connections; it was a witty riff on a meme featuring *RuPaul's Drag Race* star Sasha Colby, who set up her underdog status with the line 'I'm your favourite drag queen's favourite drag queen'. Chappell's self-deprecating quip delighted the internet so much that it even spawned a quirky Google easter egg.

For several months afterwards, whenever someone searched for Chappell's name they would receive the message: 'Did you mean: your favourite artist's favourite artist?' During an appearance on *The Tonight Show Starring Jimmy Fallon*, Chappell insisted she had nothing to do with this development. 'No, it's this random twink who works at Google, I know it is,' she told host Jimmy Fallon. 'I know it's just some assistant [who's like], "Ooh we love her!"'

Over the next few months, Chappell's profile and streaming numbers snowballed as she continued to tour North America. *The Rise and Fall of a Midwest Princess* entered the UK Official Albums Chart for the first time in late April and cracked the top 40 in early June. In May, two of its songs joined 'Good Luck, Babe!' in the UK Official Singles Chart: 'Hot to Go!' and 'Red Wine Supernova'. When Chappell performed at the Governors Ball festival in New York in June, she came on stage dressed as a drag incarnation of the Statue of Liberty: a high-camp moment that endeared her to locals. Later in her set, Chappell revealed that she had declined an invitation to perform at a White House Pride event.

> *'We want **liberty, justice** and **freedom** for all. When you do that, that's when I'll come,'*

she told the crowd. After quoting a poem etched on the Statue of Liberty, which mentions 'huddled masses, yearning to breathe free', Chappell doubled down on her demands: 'That means freedom and trans rights, that means freedom and women's rights, and it especially means freedom for all oppressed people in occupied territories.' Her set also featured the live debut of 'The Subway', a lusty new song about an intense girl crush.

CHAPPELL KEEPS SOARING

Chappell's career was soaring, but it was also beginning to give her vertigo. At a show in Raleigh, North Carolina, that fell four days after the Governors Ball, Chappell told the crowd she was 'feeling a little off' that day. 'I think my career is just kind of going really fast and it's really hard to keep up,' she said. 'This is all I've ever wanted, it's just heavy sometimes.' By this point, there was no way to put on the brakes. When she played Bonnaroo festival in Tennessee later that week, organizers had to move her to a bigger stage to meet demand. The very next day, her album entered the US top ten for the first time.

In July, a Vox headline seemed to capture her paradoxical situation perfectly: 'Chappell Roan spent 7 years becoming an overnight success.' She was still touring, still winning new fans and still struggling to keep up. When she performed at Lollapalooza festival in Chicago in August, organizers made the call to upgrade her to the main stage, but Chappell still exceeded their expectations. A spokesperson for the festival, which has a rich history dating back to the 1990s, told CNN afterwards: 'Chappell's performance was the biggest daytime set we've ever seen.' After exiting the stage to deafening applause, Chappell was comforted by pop singer Kesha, one of her musical heroes. 'It felt like a big sister was helping me through it,' she told Elle. But it must have felt strangely bittersweet, too, given that Kesha's set had been bumped off the main stage to make way for Chappell.

In the weeks after Lollapalooza, *The Rise and Fall of a Midwest Princess* climbed to number one in the UK and number two in the US. In her homeland, it was only held off the top spot by Taylor Swift's *The Tortured Poets Department*, the best-selling album of the year. This should have been a moment of unalloyed joy, but instead, Chappell was dealing with the collateral damage of success. On TikTok, she bemoaned the increasingly 'creepy' and 'entitled' behaviour of some hardcore fans, who had tracked down her sister's workplace and family's home address. 'I don't care that abuse and harassment, stalking, whatever is a normal thing to do to people who are famous or a little famous, whatever,' Chappell said firmly. 'I don't care that it's normal. I don't care that this crazy type of behaviour comes along with the job, the career field I've chosen. That does not make it OK.'

Chappell onstage at the Bonnaroo music festival in Manchester, Tennessee, in June 2024. She posted on Instagram that her spandex dress was an homage to the 2003 movie Party Monster, *a camp classic starring Macaulay Culkin.*

*'Chappell's performance was the **biggest** daytime set we've **ever seen.**'*

LOLLAPALOOZA

CHAPPELL WINS AN AWARD

Chappell was also facing some tough decisions. In late August, she told fans she was 'heartbroken' to be cancelling upcoming gigs in Paris and Amsterdam that were due to take place the following week. A third date in Berlin was postponed until later in the month. On 11 September, she returned to the stage at the MTV Video Music Awards (VMAs) in Elmont, New York, a night of triumphant highs and traumatizing lows for Chappell. On the one hand, she took home the Best New Artist trophy, which she dedicated to 'queer and trans people that fuel pop' and 'all the drag artists who inspire me'. She also delivered a scorching performance of 'Good Luck, Babe!' with a medieval knights theme, beginning the song by shooting a flaming arrow out of a crossbow to ignite the stage's pyrotechnics: a move that hit the target in all senses. But on the other hand, things got heated in a less welcome way on the red carpet. In a clip that quickly went viral, Chappell can be seen pointing at a photographer who had allegedly yelled at her. 'You shut the fuck up. No, not me, bitch,' she tells them firmly. Later that evening, Chappell told *Entertainment Tonight* that 'For someone who gets a lot of anxiety around people yelling at you, the carpet is horrifying.' Many fans applauded Chappell's decision to stick up for herself, but others accused her of being 'rude'. For the first time, she was experiencing 'tall poppy syndrome', the cultural phenomenon that imposes greater scrutiny and criticism on people who have enjoyed a sudden rise. It's a particularly cruel application of the famous saying: 'What comes up, must come down'.

After the VMAs, Chappell continued The Midwest Princess Tour in Europe, where she played sold-out shows in Manchester, Glasgow, Dublin, London and Berlin. In an interview with the *Guardian*, Chappell likened her new-found fame to 'going through puberty' again. 'My body does feel different. It's holding tension in a very different way. I have all these new emotions and I'm really confused,' she said. At the end of the month, 'Good Luck, Babe!' climbed to number four on the US Billboard Hot 100, an especially impressive peak given that it still didn't have a music video. Chappell told *Rolling Stone* that she was simply 'too tired' to make one: 'Do you know how hard it is to do a music video when you're this exhausted and burnt?'

In October, Chappell finally completed The Midwest Princess Tour after 94 dates spread over 13 months. The final stretch included her biggest headline show yet, in Council Bluffs, Iowa, where she played to a crowd of 15,000, including a sizeable LGBTQIA+ contingent. 'Yes, gay people exist in the Midwest!' Chappell told the audience jubilantly. '[In] flyover states, there are twinks in all of them! There are dolls in all of them!' Remarkably, Chappell's popularity was still growing at home and across the Atlantic. In the UK, 'Hot to Go!' became Chappell's second song to crack the UK top ten (after 'Good Luck, Babe!') and 'Pink Pony Club' stormed into the top 20. In a way, Chappell

Chappell collects her Best New Artist award at the MTV VMAs in a chainmail stage outfit inspired by Joan of Arc.

had no need to release new music because her old songs were still scaling the charts.

Still, Chappell did debut a new song called 'The Giver' during a TV performance on *Saturday Night Live* in early November. Featuring fiddles and a rollicking honky-tonk beat, this absolute banger is Chappell's first foray into country music and a joyful celebration of lesbian sex. When Chappell sings: 'so take it like a taker, 'cause baby I'm a giver,' she doesn't mean Christmas presents. During a Q&A event at the Grammy Museum a few days later, Chappell reassured fans that 'The Giver' would come out as a single in the fullness of time. She also described writing it as a full-circle moment: 'I got to bring what I knew to the table, 'cause I'm a country girl. I got to be like, "Let me show you some country songs,"' she said. Chappell eventually released 'The Giver' as a single in March 2025, trailed by a series of playfully risqué teaser images in which she dressed as a plumber and a dentist. When she shared a picture of herself holding a plumber's plunger on Facebook, Chappell wrote with an implied wink: 'Yep. Showing crack is back.'

CHAPPELL TAKES STOCK

Chappell began 2025 with another accolade when she topped BBC Radio 1's Sound of 2025 list. This annual poll coronating music's biggest rising stars is voted for by a panel of 180 experts and musicians including Dua Lipa, Sam Smith and Chappell's pal Elton John. When he announced Chappell's victory live on air, BBC Radio 1's Jack Saunders acknowledged that her star was already well in the ascendance. 'She was the most exciting artist of the last 12 months and is now set to be the artist of the next 12 months,' he told listeners. 'The success is all her own doing: standing tall in the face of the doubters and keeping her community close to fuel the energy of her shows and musical movements.' In an accompanying interview, Chappell spoke about putting the brakes on her career, or at least trying to: 'If I were to override more of my basic instincts, where my heart is going, "Stop, stop, stop, you're not OK", I would be bigger,' she said. 'I would be way bigger. And I would still be on tour right now.'

She also credited her late grandfather, Dennis Chappell, with giving her perspective and the courage to say no: 'There's something he said that I think about in every move I make with my career: "There are always options,"' Chappell said.

> *'So, when someone says, "Do this concert because you'll never get offered* ***that much money*** *ever again", it's like,* ***who cares?*** *There is not a scarcity of opportunity. I think about that* ***all the time.****'*

After her discombobulating year, Chappell was recalibrating her career firmly on her own terms. At the Grammys in early February 2025, she sang 'Pink Pony Club' while straddling a giant steed that looked like a blown up My Little Pony toy. Backed by dancers dressed as rodeo clowns, her performance was campy, colourful and completely triumphant. Later in the evening, when she collected the Best New Artist award, Chappell used her acceptance speech to call out inequalities in the music industry.

'I would ***demand*** *that labels in the industry profiting millions of dollars off of artists offer a* ***liveable wage*** *and* ***healthcare****, especially to developing artists.'*

Chappell recalled that when she was dropped by her label four years earlier, she struggled to find work and couldn't afford healthcare. 'It was so devastating to feel so committed to my art and feel so betrayed by the system and so dehumanized,' she said. This incredibly passionate speech felt like another defining moment in Chappell's stratospheric rise. After grafting for seven years to become an 'overnight' success, she hadn't forgotten the obstacles she overcame along the way.

THE GRAMMYS

★ YOUR ★ FAVOURITE *Artist's* FAVOURITE *Artists*

Chappell's Musical Influences

No musician exists in a vacuum; they all draw from their favourite songs and most cherished artists as they pour highly personal feelings into hopefully unique music and lyrics.

A great pop song can feel fresh even when it references the past – just look at the way Chappell's 'Hot to Go!' channels the chant-along spirit of Village People's disco classic 'Y.M.C.A.' – 'It's like the Y.M.C.A. but gayer is how I describe it,' Chappell told Pop Crave.

The rise of our Midwest princess was fuelled by her fascination with artists who blew her mind and expanded her horizons. When she was a teenager, the kaleidoscopic pop stars of the early 2010s introduced Chappell to an exciting new world outside conservative Willard, Missouri. 'It was impossible to escape pop music at that time because it was [so much] Katy Perry, Rihanna, Gaga and Kesha. Just every pop girly – it was massive,' Chappell told *Five Cent Sound*.

In so many of her interviews, Chappell speaks generously about the singers who inspire her – some on a strictly musical level, others in terms of how they manage their careers and interact with the world. So, here's a comprehensive guide to your favourite artist's favourite artists. In many cases, they are now Chappell's peers, mentors and even friends.

★ ALANIS ★ MORISSETTE

Chappell has described the Canadian singer-songwriter as her 'ultimate idol'. Morissette began her career as a frothy dance-pop singer before reinventing herself as the queen of female angst with her 1995 album *Jagged Little Pill*. When Chappell covered its standout single 'You Oughta Know' at live shows in 2022 and 2023, she would often tell the crowd: 'I didn't write this song, I wish I did.' Clearly, she relates to Morissette's cathartic lyrics about a truly agonizing breakup.

Since then, Chappell will hopefully have drawn strength from the empathetic way her idol has spoken about her. 'I completely understand what it's like to be inside the white-hot heat of fame and notoriety,' Morissette told *W* magazine in 2024. 'And I think about Chappell Roan right now. I think about these women who are just in it. I'm here [for them].'

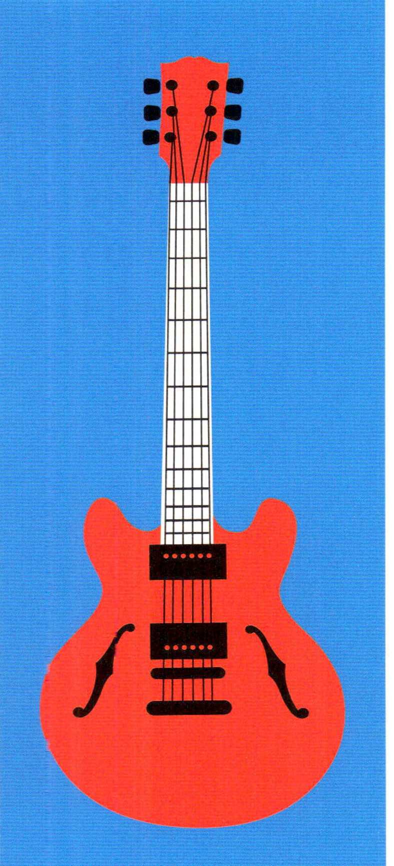

★ ALT-J ★

This British indie band have won acclaim with their inventive, genre-melding sound and clever, postmodern lyrics. They're most popular in the UK but also have a cult following in the US, where their 2012 debut album *An Awesome Wave* went platinum. Chappell told I Dream of Vinyl in 2020: 'I would love to collaborate with Alt-J. I think they're amazing.'

★ ARIANA GRANDE ★

In a 2024 interview with Billboard, Chappell called herself 'an Arianator', showing she's au fait with Grande's fanbase name. She also shared her 'love' for the singer's latest album, *Eternal Sunshine*. Later that year, Chappell revealed that Grande was her most listened to artist of 2024 according to Spotify Wrapped.

The two pop queens also have a friend in common: Bowen Yang. When the actor-comedian spoke to Chappell for *Interview* magazine, he revealed that he mentioned Chappell to Grande on the *Wicked* set. 'I remember drinking a glass of wine with Ariana Grande after we wrapped and being like, "You should get on Chappell Roan,"' he recalled. Let's hope he keeps spreading the word.

★ BEYONCÉ ★

In a 2018 interview with *Anchr* magazine, Chappell said that Queen Bey and Lady Gaga 'really inspire me with their stage presence'. She added rather presciently: 'They are both so confident and really own the stage and connect with the crowd so well. I hope to be like them one day.'

Chappell has singled out Spears and another pop star who dominated the Y2K era, Pink, as her 'early influences'. She told the *Milwaukee Journal Sentinel*: 'I didn't listen to a lot of them growing up, just here and there. I was mostly raised on Christian rock and country music.' In the same interview, Chappell said the chart hits of her childhood were a reference point when she wrote 'Hot to Go!': 'I really wanted an undeniable gay pop song, so I pulled from the greatest pop girlies and the 2000s and 2010s,' she explained.

★ BRITNEY ★ SPEARS

★ THE ★ CRANBERRIES

Led by singer Dolores O'Riordan, who sadly passed away in 2018, Irish five-piece The Cranberries were leading lights of the 1990s' alt-rock era. Chappell has never mentioned them in an interview, but we know she likes their jangly debut single, 'Dreams', because she covered it at live shows in 2018. You can watch Chappell's lovely version on YouTube – her voice really suits the lilting melodies.

★ CYNDI ★ LAUPER

With dazzling hits such as 'Girls Just Want to Have Fun' and 'Time After Time', Lauper helped to define the 1980s' new wave sound. Chappell has mentioned her in several interviews and has covered 'True Colors', Lauper's beautiful LGBTQIA+ rights anthem, at an early live show. The respect is mutual – Lauper said in 2024 that she loves Chappell for her 'hair alone'. Speaking on *Watch What Happens Live with Andy Cohen*, Lauper went on to praise the 'performance art' quality of Chappell's performances, adding: 'It's visual, so visual.'

★DRAKE★

As a teenager, Chappell drew comfort from the Canadian singer-rapper's deeply introspective music. 'I downloaded Pandora and I would sit in my bathroom and just listen to Drake,' she told *Variety*. In the same interview, she said hip-hop music generally made her feel 'really cool' and gave her somewhere to store all her 'angsty feelings'.

★ ELLIE ★ GOULDING

Chappell told Pop Crave that she listened to this British pop singer, who is known for her floaty vocal style, throughout her high school years. She covered one of her songs, the shimmering electro gem 'Lights', at a live show in 2012.

★ ELTON JOHN ★

Sir Elton Hercules John, to use his full name, has really taken Chappell under his wing. The two musicians grabbed pizza together in June 2024 and he's given her some sterling songwriting advice. 'The advice he gave me was that the songs will come,' Chappell told *TIME* magazine. 'He thought that he wouldn't have the ideas, but they were absolutely there. He just had to let them come to him. So that's a good reminder.'

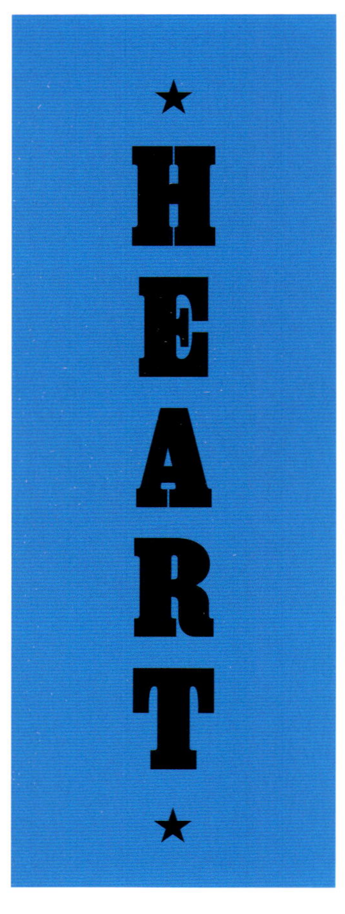

When Chappell shared her Spotify Wrapped results in December 2024, she revealed that Heart's 1977 hit 'Barracuda' was her most played song of the year. She also covered this blistering rock anthem on two dates of her Midwest Princess Tour.

Heart's two female members, sisters Ann and Nancy Wilson, wrote 'Barracuda' in response to music industry sexism and a tasteless publicity stunt concocted by their record label. Chappell has never specified why she loves this song, but the lyrics about a ruthless executive 'lying so low in the weeds' are definitely evocative. Like every major artist, Chappell will almost certainly have encountered a few barracudas while building her career.

★ JOAN JETT ★

Cool, confident and uncompromising, Jett has earned her bragging rights as the 'queen of rock and roll'. With 1980s' anthems like 'Bad Reputation' and 'Victim of Circumstance', she helped to dismantle the sexist notion that playing rough, tough hard rock is only a job for the boys.

During her 2024 appearance on *The Comment Section with Drew Afualo* podcast, Chappell called herself a Joan Jett 'fangirl' and said she loves Googling images of the singer. 'I think if I didn't have a job, she would become my job in life,' she admitted. Chappell told *Rolling Stone* a few months later: 'Anything that I listen to – Joan Jett, Heart, Gaga – I want to feel like them. So I'll just be inspired by that feeling and how I can capture it.'

Accompanied by her brother Richard, the late Karen Carpenter delivered hauntingly pure vocal performances on a string of 1970s' hits including '(They Long to Be) Close to You', 'Yesterday Once More' and 'Please Mr Postman'. In a 2018 interview with *Anchr* magazine, Chappell cited Carpenter and Fleetwood Mac singer Stevie Nicks as her 'main vocal influences'. As ever, there's no denying her impeccable taste.

★ KAREN ★ CARPENTER

★ KATE BUSH ★

This famously mysterious musician ranks among the most unique and influential artists of the 1970s and 1980s. In 2022, she beguiled a new generation of fans when her 1985 single 'Running Up That Hill' featured prominently in *Stranger Things*. In several interviews, Chappell has cited Bush as a major influence on her own distinctive music. On YouTube, you can find fan-made mash-ups of 'Running Up That Hill' and Chappell's synth-pop banger 'Good Luck, Babe!'. The two songs blend together in a pretty magical way.

★ KATY ★ PERRY

At a formative age, Chappell was drawn to the radio-slaying anthems on Perry's 2010 album *Teenage Dream*, home to smashes including 'Firework' and 'California Gurls'. 'Oh my god, *Teenage Dream* came out when I was 13. Like, it was just perfect pop,' she said in a 2024 interview with *NME*. Since then, Perry has repaid the compliment by telling BBC Radio 2: 'I relate to Chappell the most because she's just so authentically herself.'

This fun and flashy artist broke through with her 2009 single 'Tik Tok', which features the indelible lyric: 'Before I leave, [I] brush my teeth with a bottle of Jack'. Chappell, who was 11 when the song came out, mentioned Kesha as a musical influence in her 2024 interview with *NME*.

In a subsequent interview with *Elle*, Chappell name-checked her again, saying: 'Kesha has always stood up for women and what she believes in, and that's very inspiring.' She also revealed that Kesha was 'so lovely' to her at Chicago's Lollapalooza music festival, where Chappell played to a record-breaking number of people. 'Because with that huge of a crowd, maybe only five other people there understood what that's like,' Chappell said.

Known for her Sam Smith collaboration 'Unholy' and a string of sleek, sex-positive club bops, Petras is especially popular with queer pop fans. In her 2024 *NME* interview, Chappell said her new music could be influenced by the spoken-word parts on Petras's 2022 EP *Slut Pop*. 'She's kind of like talk-singing and I just feel like I need to do that,' she said. It's a vocal style Chappell has experimented with on her *Midwest Princess* banger 'Super Graphic Ultra Modern Girl'.

★ KIM ★ PETRAS

★ LANA DEL REY ★

Pop's modern-day queen of mystique has been a major artist since Chappell was a teenager. In a 2024 interview with *Nylon*, Chappell revealed that Del Rey is her most-played artist of all time. It makes sense, then, that she name-checks her on this lyric from 'Naked in Manhattan': 'When I sing that Lana song, it makes you cry.' During a TikTok Live chat, Chappell said the Lana songs that make her cry are 'Ride', a soulful ballad, and the psychedelic country gem 'Mariners Apartment Complex'.

★ LADY GAGA ★

The artist fans call 'Mother Monster' has been a huge influence on Chappell. When MTV asked her to name the music video that changed her life, Chappell picked Gaga's 'Alejandro' because 'I had not seen the things that she was doing in that video before'. Chappell is also a massive fan of Gaga's song 'Bad Romance', which she covered at 40 shows on The Midwest Princess Tour.

What's more, Chappell isn't the only member of her family to love Gaga. During her appearance on 'A Carpool Karaoke Christmas', Chappell revealed that her dad named a chicken – yes, really – after the singer. When this clip was shared on TikTok, Gaga left a comment calling it 'an honor, truly' to have an avian namesake. Chappell will surely have blushed when she saw this!

★ LORDE ★

Chappell listened to Lorde throughout her high school years. The New Zealand artist, who scored her breakthrough hit 'Royals' when she was just 16, has since acted as something of a mentor. In her 2024 interview with *The Face*, Chappell revealed that she texted Lorde after two male fans harassed her at an airport. 'She sent me a list of things I should do – literally wrote down eight things she wished someone would have told her when she was going through it,' Chappell said. Clearly she appreciates having Lorde in her corner.

★ MADONNA ★

Some music fans have compared Chappell to the longtime 'queen of pop', even branding her 'the Gen Z Madonna'. Chappell has never shared her thoughts on this comparison, but she did tell *Illustrate Magazine*: 'My strongest influence is definitely 80s synth-pop. I love weird sounds. I love dance and anthemic pop. Queen and Madonna vibes.' Could she cover a Madonna classic one day? We'd love to see it.

When Cyrus was named a Disney Legend in 2024, Chappell recorded a sweet video message. She revealed that the first pop concert she ever went to was Cyrus's Best of Both Worlds Tour, in which Cyrus performed as both herself and her TV alter ego Hannah Montana. 'She came down in a box from the ceiling. I was like, "How do I do that one day?" I still think about it,' Chappell recalled.

In the same message, Chappell admitted that 'there's a lot of crossover between Miley' and her own project. 'The things that I admire about Miley Cyrus is that she constantly reinvents herself and it always works,' Chappell said. 'For a lot of artists, it can seem inauthentic or out of the blue, but she's very open about her transformations artistically and personally. She's so true to herself.'

★ MILEY CYRUS ★

This wildly charismatic rapper made a splash with her 2010 debut *Pink Friday*, home to the perky pop-rap hits 'Check It Out' and 'Super Bass'. Chappell cited the *Pink Friday* era as an influence during her 2024 *NME* interview.

★ NICKI ★ MINAJ

★ OLIVIA ★ RODRIGO

As we already know, Chappell's career is closely intertwined with Rodrigo's. Thanks to their shared producer, Dan Nigro, Chappell sang backing vocals on Rodrigo's songs 'Lacy', 'Obsessed' and 'Can't Catch Me Now'.

Then, in 2024, Rodrigo asked Chappell to open for her on the *GUTS* World Tour, which brought the *Midwest Princess* singer to a wider audience. 'I am so excited and very grateful to Olivia – she is an angel,' Chappell told *NME* ahead of the tour. 'I'm just not really sure how it's gonna feel to do an arena show!' At a *GUTS* concert in Los Angeles, Chappell joined Olivia for a duet rendition of 'Hot to Go!', a memorable moment you can check out on YouTube.

★ QUEEN ★

In 2018, the Oscar-winning biopic *Bohemian Rhapsody* introduced this flamboyant British rock band to a new generation of fans. Chappell was struck by a scene in which frontman Freddie Mercury, played by Rami Malek, gets an entire stadium clapping along to Queen's 1984 smash 'Radio Ga Ga'. 'That changed my career,' she said during an interview at the Grammy Museum. 'I just thought to myself, "How do I do something [where] I can look out and have everyone do the same thing like that?" It was so powerful.'

★ RENEÉ RAPP ★

Like Chappell, singer and actress Reneé Rapp is injecting pop culture with an overdue dose of authentic queer female sexuality. The two artists have a lot in common, so it's heartening to hear that they respect each other's art. 'I met her for the first time at a party this weekend,' Chappell told *Nylon* in 2024. 'She held both my hands so tight. She was like, "You don't understand how big a fan I am of yours. I love you so much." I was like, "Oh my god. Same."' Fans have been manifesting a collaboration ever since.

★ RIHANNA ★

These days, Rihanna is the billionaire businesswoman behind Fenty Beauty. But when Chappell was a teenager, Rihanna was one of the world's biggest and most electrifying pop stars. When Rihanna released a stunning, stripped-down ballad called 'Stay' in 2012, Chappell was inspired to write music of her own. A year later, Chappell covered 'Stay' at one of her first live shows.

Nicks is so legendary that she's been inducted into the Rock and Roll Hall of Fame twice: first as a member of seminal rock band Fleetwood Mac and then as a solo artist. Chappell, who hails Nicks as a major vocal influence, has covered her Fleetwood Mac song 'Dreams' at a handful of live shows.

The respect travels both ways. In October 2024, Nicks praised Chappell for putting her health and wellbeing ahead of work commitments. 'Me and a friend of mine went and looked at her schedule, and it was outrageous,' Nicks told *Rolling Stone*. 'They'll burn her out if that's what they want to do, because there's always somebody to replace you. It must make them all very fearful. That's why it's good that Chappell just said, "Well, go ahead, replace me. I'm cancelling because I'm not going to drop dead for all you people."'

These days, Chappell is earning serious plaudits from the iconic artists she grew up listening to.

★ STEVIE ★ NICKS

★ A ★ KALEIDOSCOPE OF *Inspiration*

Drag and Queer Representation in Chappell's Work

Pearl

In December 2023, Chappell played two headline shows at Heaven, London's most iconic LGBTQIA+ venue.

It's a vast, cavernous space under Charing Cross train station where queer icons like Boy George, Freddie Mercury and Divine used to party back in the 1980s. These days, it regularly hosts performances by the superstar queens of *RuPaul's Drag Race*. 'That was so affirming for me because Heaven is famously so joyous,' Chappell told me when I interviewed her for *NME*.

During one of her nights at Heaven, Chappell had a revelation while she was getting stage-ready in the bijou upstairs dressing room. Crayola, a local drag queen booked to open the show, saw Chappell putting on her makeup and said: 'Oh, you are a drag queen.' Initially, Chappell struggled to accept the compliment. On Tom Power's podcast, she recalled telling Crayola: 'Oh, you know, I'm like you. I need to get my makeup and my clothes on and kind of transform.' To which Crayola replied: 'Honey, you are a drag queen.'

For Chappell, this was an 'altering' and validating exchange. 'There was something that switched,' she told Tom Power. 'I really have taken that on as an identity and it's been very freeing to be like, "Oh, Chappell Roan is my drag project."' Still, even since this lightning-bolt moment, Chappell very much puts drag acts on a pedestal. When *RuPaul's Drag Race* star Trixie Mattel interviewed Chappell for *Paper* magazine in June 2024, she declared her the 'missing link' between pop stars and drag queens. Chappell replied modestly: 'I would not even make the finals at a local [drag] show. I can't really give shows the way that actual queens can.'

Despite Chappell's lingering hints of imposter syndrome, the drag community definitely sees her as one of their own. Inga Rock, a London-based queen who also opened for Chappell at Heaven, told me excitedly: 'We love her! It's like someone from our team has gone and made it. When one of us wins, we all win.' Tequila Thirst (pictured left), a queen who opened for Chappell in Manchester in September 2024, was equally effusive: 'You can tell Chappell has a real grounding on the drag scene,' Tequila told me. 'She's spent time in the places where we perform, so she knows exactly how we feel and what we do. She's one of us.'

Chappell's fascination with drag began in 2018, shortly after she moved from the Midwest to Los Angeles. When she stepped into The Abbey, the multi-room LGBTQIA+ venue that has its own pastry shop and a nightclub space called The Chapel, it must have felt too good to be true. 'It was shortly after I had turned 21 and I could finally go out. The Abbey was packed, there were go-go dancers on the table, and I walked in and it was the most spiritual experience,' Chappell told *Headliner* magazine. 'Everyone was having a great time; it was magical. I just felt like I belonged there, and that really changed my life.' Chappell poured this transformative experience into 'Pink Pony Club', her 2020 single about a Tennessee girl who becomes a go-go dancer at a club 'where there are lovers in the bathroom and a line outside the door'. Wonderfully upbeat and colourful in comparison to her earlier dark-pop material, this euphoric song took Chappell's career in a new, more overtly queer direction.

Of course, she didn't just turn into a drag queen overnight – it took time for Chappell to weave drag's transgressive glamour and gender-bending aesthetic into her work. When she released her 'Pink Pony Club' music video in April 2020, she left the drag looks to her co-stars Meatball and Pork Chop. Wearing natural-looking makeup and a fringe sequin jacket, Chappell looks more like a campy country singer. But after she was dropped by Atlantic Records in August of that year, her image began to blossom with her music. With no major label guidance – and more importantly, no major label budget – she had to get creative.

Out of necessity, she became a self-styled 'thrift-store pop star' and 'DIY queen' who made her own tour costumes and painted her own face. She also embraced the anything-goes potential of drag. In 2022's 'Femininomenon' music video, which she filmed in her parents' backyard in Missouri, Chappell rides a bedazzled version of her father's dirt bike in a pair of customized pink assless chaps. In other scenes, we see Chappell paying homage to drag icon Divine, with pencil-thin eyebrows painted in a wickedly high arch. Chappell paid tribute to Divine again two years later during her performance at Kentuckiana Pride. This time, she wore a form-fitting scarlet dress inspired by Divine's signature outfit from the cult 1972 movie *Pink Flamingos*. When she shared photos of the look on Instagram, Chappell quoted a famous line from the film: 'Filth is my politics! Filth is my life!'

Chappell took care of her own makeup until April 2024, when she worked with professional makeup artist Doniella Davy for the first time at Coachella. 'I love it. I don't have to carry anything [anymore],' Chappell told Trixie Mattel a few months later. Davy has since mentioned that Boy George and *RuPaul's Drag Race* star Violet Chachki are key reference points for Chappell's makeup, which she described as 'drag-inspired, campy [and] kitschy'. Discussing Chappell's aesthetic generally, Davy told Fashionista: 'It's all about not giving a shit and just doing what she thinks is fun. It's not overthinking it. She just wants to do what will bring her joy, what inspires her, and she wants to be an example in that way.'

Chappell channels Divine's character in Pink Flamingos, *an infamous criminal who calls herself Babs Johnson. Upon its release in 1972, the provocative film was marketed as 'an exercise in poor taste'.*

GIVING BACK TO THE DRAG COMMUNITY

When Chappell embarked on her first headline tour in February 2023, she booked local drag queens to open for her at every show. 'I remember thinking, like, I have to do this,' Chappell said when I interviewed her for *NME*. 'So we just made a submission form with questions like: "Show us your TikTok, show us your Instagram, can you do intimate pop?" And we got submissions from queens in every city.'

On that first tour, she received the highest number of applications from queens in Toronto and Salt Lake City; the latter came as a surprise to Chappell, given the city's 'very Mormon' reputation. Later that year, she told *DIY* magazine that booking drag acts isn't simply an 'exciting' addition to her live show; it's also her way of creating 'a safe space for queer people'. Many drag queens who open for Chappell will step out in front of the largest crowd of their career to date. Inga Rock told me: 'Opportunities like this don't always come around for trans girls like me, so I still feel incredibly grateful to Chappell.'

Chappell and her team have made the application process as easy as possible. 'In terms of what I'm looking for, it's the outfits, their energy on stage, what songs they choose, their dancing. I just want someone who can really bring it,' she said in her *NME* interview. Drag artist and performer CJ Banks told me she wasn't 'particularly familiar with Chappell's work' when she applied to open for her in Glasgow last September. She only found out about the opportunity

because so many local queens were posting about it. 'The last question on the form was something like, "If you could recommend someone other than yourself to open for Chappell, please write their name here,"' CJ recalled. 'It was like a peer review system, so of course every queen was sharing it on their Instagram Story.' CJ's friends convinced her to apply, but she figured her chances were slim because of Glasgow's deep talent pool.

However, nine days before The Midwest Princess Tour arrived in town, CJ received an email with a booking offer. Chappell was looking for a 'high-energy pop number' lasting between five and eight minutes, entirely lip-synced and ideally featuring 'multiple songs' in a medley. As a guide, the email included a list of Chappell's favourite artists: Lady Gaga, Beyoncé, Britney Spears, Rihanna and Katy Perry. CJ said she appreciated this clear brief because she usually sings live, so she planned a lip-sync to three Kylie Minogue bangers. 'It went down very well on the night,' she recalled. 'I have some tricks up my sleeve, so I threw in cartwheels, forward rolls and handstands. I also got to introduce the other drag queens on the bill, which was fabulous.'

Every drag performer I spoke to shared overwhelmingly positive memories of opening for Chappell. 'It wasn't like doing drag for straight people, which is a lot of my work these days,' CJ Banks said. 'It was very much a queer audience who appreciated the art form we were putting on stage.' Tequila Thirst said that when she opened for Chappell in Manchester, the singer thanked her with a surprise shout-out.

*'She told the crowd: "**This is why I'm here** – because of performers like Tequila Thirst." I was **literally crying** on the floor!'*

Chappell also spent time with Tequila and the other queens backstage. 'She had literally just flown in from the VMAs [in New York], which was absolutely huge, so she didn't have to make an effort,' Tequila recalled. 'But she still had a good chat with us for, like, ten to fifteen minutes. She was a little shy but so, so lovely.'

Chappell is also acutely aware of the financial pressures faced by drag queens in the current economic climate. In Manchester, she used a Tequila Thirst-branded fan throughout her performance, effectively giving the queen's merchandise an extended plug. Inga Rock said that Chappell's team asked for her Paypal details right after the show – a state of affairs that sadly isn't industry standard. 'She also made a point of reminding the audience to tip us,' Inga added.

> *'That was* ***special****, because she didn't need to – she was already paying us. And I got so many cute messages with my tips like, "***Chappell made me do it!***"'*

This isn't the only way Chappell pays it back. Since she began playing headline shows in 2023, she has donated a portion of ticket sales to For the Gworls, a New York charity that helps Black trans folk with rent, gender-affirmative surgeries and medical needs. She also donates to The Trevor Project, a charity working to reduce suicide rates among LGBTQIA+ young people, and The GLO Center, a queer community group in Missouri. 'I don't advertise that as much anymore, but it's still daily. It's still part of every ticket I sell,' Chappell told *Revue* magazine in May 2024. As part of her mission 'to uplift the queer community', Chappell also mentioned her 'scholarship programme where I can offer people tickets who can't afford them'. She recognizes the importance of platforming queer culture because finding a safe space at The Abbey had such a profound effect on her. 'It's sick to sell merch and whatever, and to sell out shows, but I really just want to hire local drag queens,' she told Revue. 'I'm not even trying to peacock right now. I genuinely just want to throw parties for gay people in small towns that don't get it.'

Pearl

QUEERING THE MAINSTREAM

Chappell has also cemented her bond with the LGBTQIA+ community by writing authentically about her queer journey. On Reddit, there's a lengthy thread where fans ponder the question: 'What do you think is Chappell's gayest song?' The answer is probably a matter of personal preference, but certain tracks jump to the front of the queue. On 'Naked in Manhattan', Chappell captures all the excitement and anticipation of sleeping with a woman for the first time. 'Could go to hell but we'll probably be fine,' she sings, batting away any lingering shame from her strict Christian upbringing. 'This song relates to having a crush on a girl or, like, a queer relationship at the beginning,' Chappell told journalist Bonnie Orbison. 'It's similar to the way that New York City makes me feel, which is, like, excited and kind of [filled with] wanderlust.' It's a sensation any queer person will remember well.

Other Chappell bangers resonate with bi and pansexual fans in particular. On 'After Midnight', which Chappell described in a Capital Buzz interview as 'a bubbly pop song' about partying, she sings about wanting to kiss 'your girlfriend' *and* 'your boyfriend'. But on 'Super Graphic Ultra Modern Girl', she's beginning to realize that her tastes may not fall straight down the middle. Over a pumping club beat, she declares that she's 'through with all these hyper mega bummer boys like you' and instead wants 'a super graphic ultra modern girl like me'. The pre-chorus really captures Chappell's growing confidence in her sexuality: 'Not overdramatic, I know what I want.'

Thrillingly, she isn't afraid to be overtly sexual in her music, either. 'Want me to fuck you? Baby, I will 'cause I really want to,' she sings on 'Red Wine Supernova', a song that also contains a cheeky come-on: 'Let's make this bed get squeaky!' Chappell's 2025 single 'The Giver' features her most intriguing exploration of lesbian sexuality yet. When she sings: 'take it like a taker, 'cause baby I'm a giver', she's presumably alluding to her role as the 'top', or dominant sexual partner. Either way, she makes it clear that she knows how to satisfy a woman: 'Ain't no country boy quitter, I get the job done!' Along with peers like Billie Eilish, Renée Rapp and Janelle Monáe, Chappell is helping to reframe queer female sexuality in pop music away from the male gaze.

Even one of Chappell's frothiest pop songs, 'Hot to Go!', contains multiple layers of queer subtext. On a superficial level, its chants and dance routine hark back to the Village People's 'Y.M.C.A.', a 1970s' disco hit that became an enduring gay anthem. But on a slightly deeper level, Chappell's decision to dress as a cheerleader in the music video feels rather radical. The high school cheerleader is often portrayed as a paragon of 'wholesome' – by which society means cisgender and hetero – female sexuality. When an openly queer artist like Chappell adopts this trope, it instantly becomes more subversive. Chappell has never spoken about putting a queer spin on cheerleader iconography, but she has said she wanted to be a cheerleader in high school. 'I just never felt like I was that kind of girl,' she added regretfully. Now she's making up for lost time in an empowering way.

But, hearteningly, Chappell's most popular song – her first to achieve a billion Spotify streams – might also be her gayest. On 'Good Luck, Babe!', she paints a poignant portrait of a woman who is desperately trying to deny her queerness. 'You can kiss a hundred boys in bars, shoot another shot, try to stop the feeling,' Chappell sings on the chorus, before underlining the futility of these efforts: 'You'd have to stop the world just to stop the feeling.' Later in the song, Chappell imagines the woman in the future, married to a man and realizing her mistake. 'You're standing face to face with "I told you so,"' she sings with a sigh. The result is a beautifully bittersweet LGBTQIA+ anthem. 'It was originally called "Good Luck, Jane!", but my co-writer and I kept getting into arguments about it. So, it became "Good Luck, Babe!"' Chappell told French music and culture website Konbini.

Chappell is also moving the dial forward by speaking candidly about her sexuality in interviews. 'She doesn't diminish her queerness to become more successful, but she doesn't tokenize it either,' CJ Banks told me. 'It never feels like she's trying to curate her image or personality for anyone else. She's just being herself.' In her 2024 interview with Capital Buzz, Chappell admitted that she still worries she isn't 'gay enough' and doesn't 'belong' in the LGBTQIA+ community. She also offered advice to young people who are dealing with similar feelings: 'I would say "be gentle". I think it took me a second to really wrap my head around queerness,' she said. 'I think that's the case for every queer person, that it's stages of, "Oh, this is who I am." "Oh actually, it's not." Or "maybe I'm not just bi, maybe I am more than bi, maybe I'm pan."' Chappell understands that coming out is an ongoing journey, not a one-time destination.

At a concert in Cleveland, Ohio, in May 2024, Chappell confirmed that she now identifies as a lesbian – previously, she had always described herself as 'queer'. She told *Rolling Stone* a few months later: 'I just wasn't supposed to be sleeping with men, and now I'm a little repulsed at the thought of even kissing a guy because no one's going to be as good as girls.' Will her sexuality continue to evolve in the future? Only time will tell. But whatever happens next, there's no doubt she'll explore it honestly and entertainingly in her music. And hopefully, with some fabulous new drag looks too.

YASSS

★ MY ★ KINK IS *Chappell*

Her Most Iconic Looks, On and Off Stage

THE TONIGHT SHOW
STARRING

Chappell Roan's stage and red carpet looks are an absolutely integral part of her project.

By dressing as a drag incarnation of the Statue of Liberty or a bedazzled medieval knight, Chappell whisks us away from everyday life and into a hyper-real fantasy world. She loves serving high camp, but she doesn't do high fashion or high street – pretty much everything she wears is bespoke. 'All the money [I make] goes to the world-building,' Chappell told *Rolling Stone* in 2024. 'That's why I am saying no to every fucking brand deal right now, because I'm like, "Does it fit in this world?" No, H&M does not fit in this world.'

Since May 2023, she has created her iconic looks with LA-based stylist Genesis Webb, whose first assignment was giving Chappell a glamorous burlesque makeover for the 'Red Wine Supernova' cover art. These close collaborators are constantly sharing ideas on WhatsApp. '[We] pull from drag, we pull from horror movies, we pull from burlesque, we pull from theatre,' Chappell explained on *The Tonight Show Starring Jimmy Fallon*. 'I love looking pretty and scary. Or, like, pretty and tacky. Or just not pretty. I love that too.'

Chappell also told Jimmy Fallon that her fashion 'isn't that serious'. It definitely isn't meant to be super-fancy or unattainable – she has cited 'gas station vibes' and the 'tackiness' of Midwestern charity shops as a style influence. 'For example, the pink pony [I rode] on the Grammys is very much kind of a knock-off My Little Pony,' she told online magazine *Them*. 'I really like knock-off stuff for some reason.' But at the same time, she and Webb put a lot of thought and effort into every single fit. With this in mind, here's a guide to Chappell's ten most iconic looks, plus the dressing-up themes she sets at her live shows.

1

CHAPPELL'S MAJORETTE *Slay*

Chappell debuted this blue-sequin majorette outfit in 2023's 'Hot to Go!' music video. She loved it so much, evidently, that she donned it again a year later at Outside Lands festival in San Francisco. With its gold epaulettes, matching sash and cute star details, it's a signature Chappell look that combines showbiz sparkle with a striking silhouette and a dash of camp. Frankly, it's worth every dollar of the dry-cleaning bill.

2

CHAPPELL SERVES *snout*

In February 2024, Chappell attended a Grammys afterparty in an elegant scarlet gown and matching headdress. Her look was partly inspired by a 19th-century opera, *The Tales of Hoffmann*, but with a significant twist: Chappell had a pig's snout like Christina Ricci in the 2006 movie *Penelope*. 'For the prosthetic nose, we were grappling with a lot of different ideas,' Webb told Vulture. 'She was like, "Let's do *Penelope*." I don't know if it's my secret to tell why she chose it. That one felt right for a variety of reasons.'

CINCHED FOR THE GODDESSES

When Chappell appeared on *The Late Show with Stephen Colbert* in February 2024, it was the first time she 'had any actual budget', according to Webb. Inspired by the Emma Stone movie *Poor Things*, Chappell's look had a romantic vibe because the episode was airing right after Valentine's Day. Her antique corset came from LA costume store The Palace and her bows were made by Mexican designer Moños de mi Niñez. It's pretty but slightly OTT: a classic Chappell combination.

CHAPPELL *says* 'EAT ME'

For her first performance at Coachella music festival in April 2024, Chappell wore a latex T-shirt featuring a provocative slogan: 'eat me'. According to Webb, this was a reference to David LaChapelle's famous 2004 photograph of Paris Hilton, in which the heiress's bikini spells out the message: 'eat the rich'. Chappell's studded choker and bracelet, which add a dark, campy edge to the look, were borrowed from the drag performer Violet Chachki.

EAT
ME

STATUE ★ OF ★ LIBERTY, *but make it drag*

When Chappell strutted on stage at the Governors Ball festival in June 2024, she told the crowd she was 'in drag' as 'the biggest queen of them all'. Naturally, Chappell's homage to the New York landmark had a provocative twist. Along with head-to-toe body paint, she wore a strapless latex top, assless chaps and a studded latex skirt, giving this look a hint of fetishware. On this occasion, Chappell's kink wasn't so much karma as a world-famous symbol of American freedom.

6

TWO SWANS *for the price of* ONE

Chappell rocked a pair of complementary looks when she appeared on *The Tonight Show* in June 2024. For her interview with host Jimmy Fallon, she evoked a black swan with oversized feathers; then for her performance, she slipped into a white swan tutu. Webb told *The New York Times* she wanted to make Chappell 'glamorous' but also 'ugly and confusing' to viewers. 'It looks scary, almost like it could be in a horror film,' she explained.

7

CHAPPELL ENTERS HER WRESTLER *Era*

Chappell made history at Lollapalooza in August 2024 when she drew the biggest daytime crowd in the festival's history. She treated fans to a visual extravaganza by filling the stage with a wrestling ring and bodybuilders lifting weights. Her own look pulled from lucha libre, a popular form of wrestling in Mexico that involves wearing a mask to hide your identity. Her pink, blue and silver bodysuit doesn't just look cool; it's probably a nod to the trans flag.

8

A KNIGHT ★ TO ★ REMEMBER

At the MTV Video Music Awards in September 2024, Chappell sang 'Good Luck, Babe!' dressed as a campy, chainmail-clad medieval knight. Webb told *Interview* magazine that Chappell's military outfit was actually 'a dress made of beautiful silver plates' and had to be changed three times to meet fire regulations. 'It was this intensively theatrical moment showing her femininity, but also the power that she holds,' Webb added.

THE RAUCOUS RODEO *Clown*

At the 2025 Grammys, Chappell sang 'Pink Pony Club' flanked by dancing rodeo clowns. She looked majestic in a custom bodysuit made by LA designer Zana Bayne, who embellished the chocolate brown leather with crystal rivets and clown face appliqué. Clowns are a recurring visual motif for Chappell, with an empowering message. 'There were a few people – mostly boys in my high school – that would call gay people clowns,' she said on Hulu's *Faces of Music*. 'So I started doing white makeup because I was like, "If you're going to call me a clown, then I'm going to be the best clown you've ever seen."'

CHAPPELL'S TOUR THEMES DECODED

★ THEME 1 ★

MERMAID

★ THEME 2 ★

MIDWEST PRINCESS

Getting dressed up is a completely joyful part of the Chappell live experience. It's an opportunity to showcase your creativity and maybe even dabble in drag. It also massively adds to the sense of community. Drag queen Tequila Thirst told me that when she opened for Chappell in Manchester, fans in the queue were complimenting each other's outfits and sharing design tips. 'One girl made a massive jellyfish outfit that I now wear in my live shows – she was kind enough to give it to me after the concert,' Tequila said. During her last UK tour, Chappell designated one of four themes for each show, so here's a handy guide in case she uses them again. Of course, they're also a great basis for a Chappell-themed party or Halloween look.

★ THEME 3 ★ MY KINK IS KARMA

★ THEME 4 ★ PINK PONY CLUB

★ THEME 1 ★

MERMAID

This theme references Chappell's 'Casual' music video, in which she falls for a sea siren played by actress Mika Leshā. Chappell called the clip a 'gay' version of the 2006 teen movie *Aquamarine*, so that's a great starting point. Think flowy fabrics in aqueous shades like teal, turquoise and sapphire, complemented by shimmering blue eyeshadow. And, if you can make a fin it's possible to walk in, so much the better.

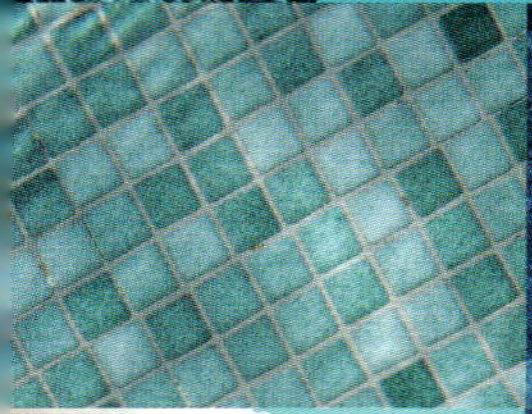

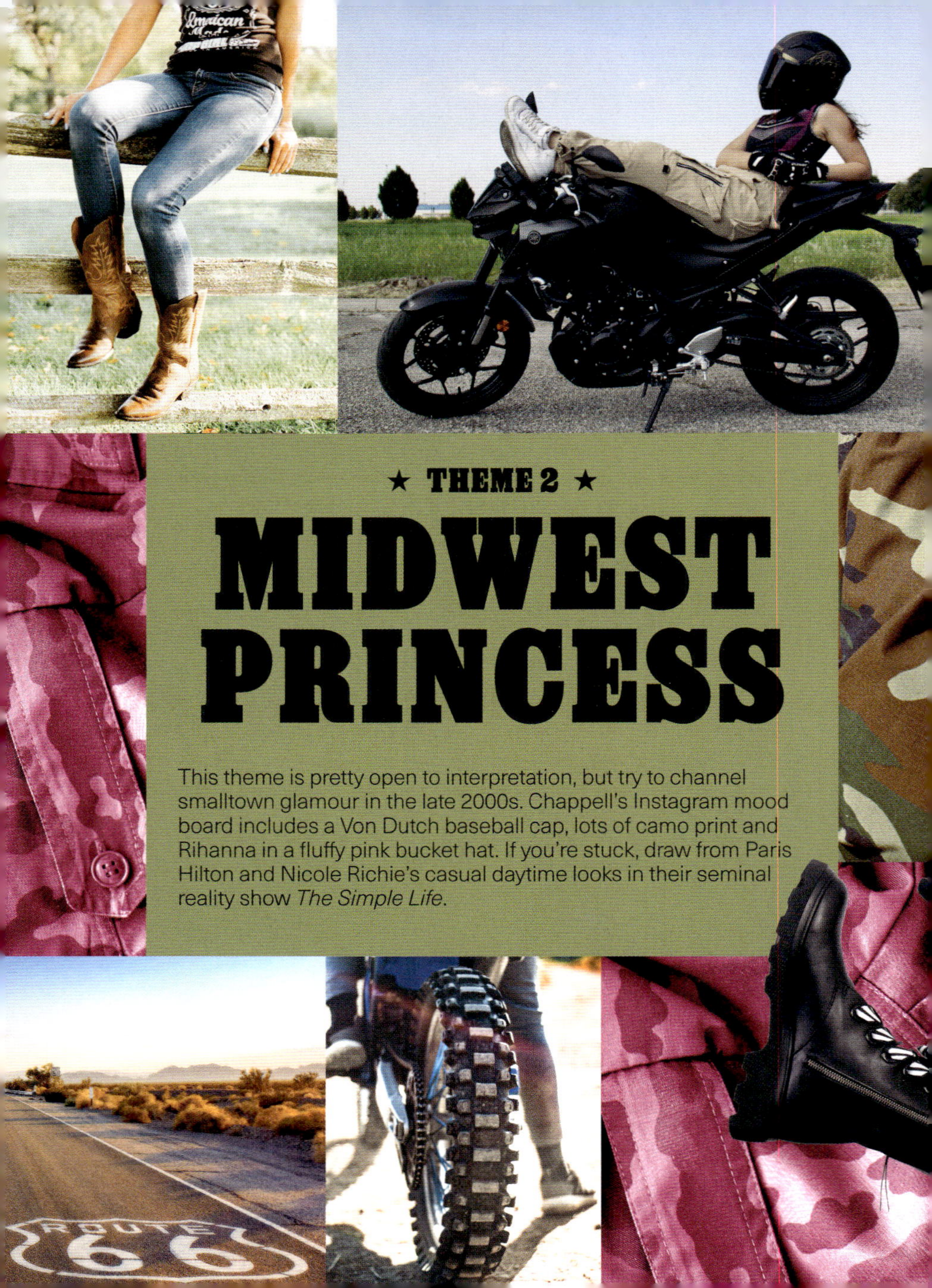

★ THEME 2 ★

MIDWEST PRINCESS

This theme is pretty open to interpretation, but try to channel smalltown glamour in the late 2000s. Chappell's Instagram mood board includes a Von Dutch baseball cap, lots of camo print and Rihanna in a fluffy pink bucket hat. If you're stuck, draw from Paris Hilton and Nicole Richie's casual daytime looks in their seminal reality show *The Simple Life*.

59

★ THEME 3 ★

MY KINK IS KARMA

In her 'My Kink Is Karma' music video and cover art, Chappell has a white heart-shaped face, bright blue eyeshadow and black devil horns. 'I didn't want it to be like a beauty shot necessarily. I wanted it to look kind of scary,' she told INTO. Use this as the basis for the tour theme: it's an opportunity to unleash your inner rock star with a fetishwear flourish.

Love

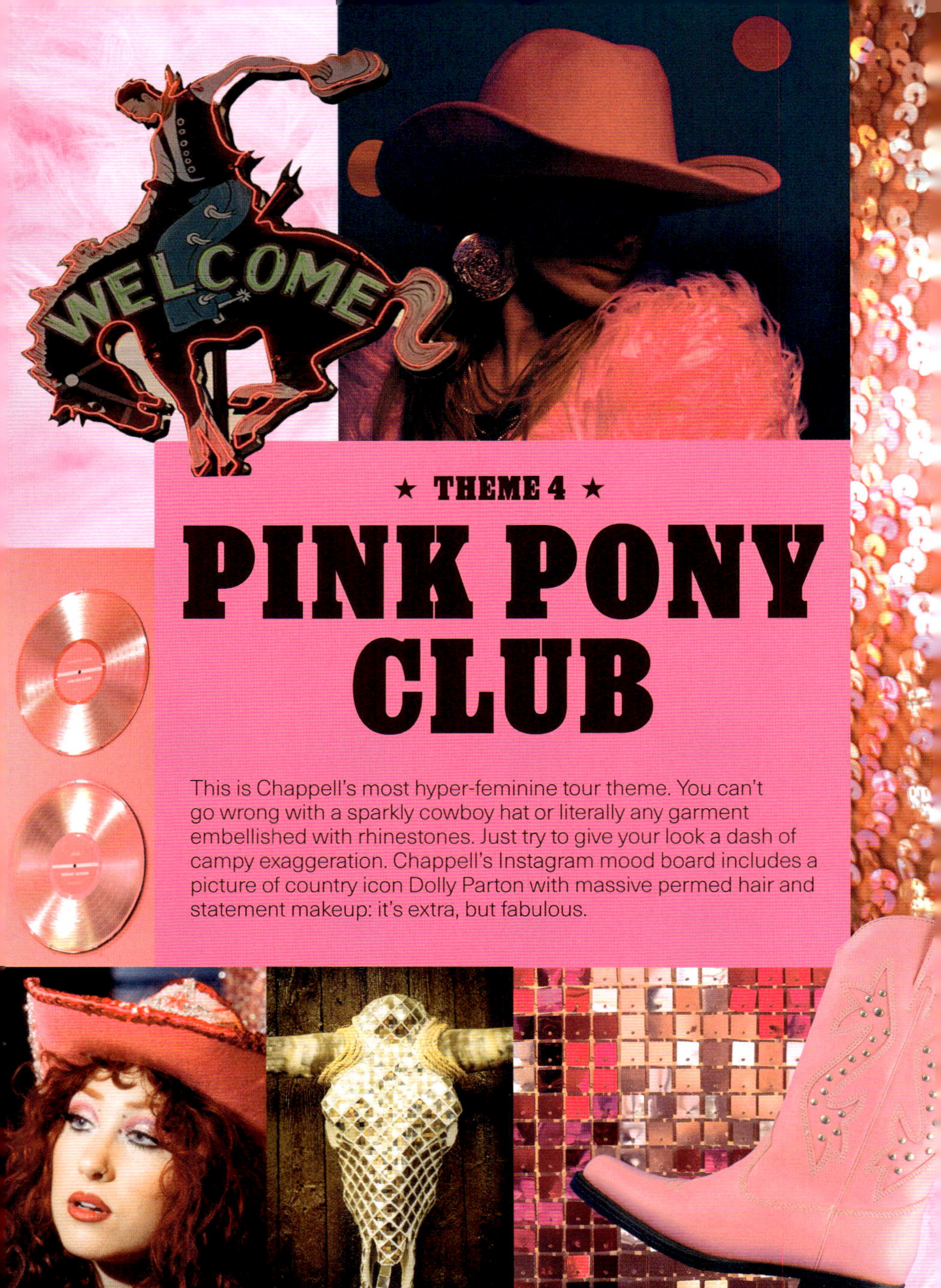

★ THEME 4 ★

PINK PONY CLUB

This is Chappell's most hyper-feminine tour theme. You can't go wrong with a sparkly cowboy hat or literally any garment embellished with rhinestones. Just try to give your look a dash of campy exaggeration. Chappell's Instagram mood board includes a picture of country icon Dolly Parton with massive permed hair and statement makeup: it's extra, but fabulous.

PINK
VIBES
ONLY

SUPER ICONIC

Ultra Famous

GIRL

Chappell's Response to Fame

As Chappell's career continued to snowball throughout 2024, she went from a cult figure – 'your favourite artist's favourite artist', as she quipped at Coachella in April – to a genuine Femininomenon.

By June, 'Good Luck, Babe!' was scaling charts all over the world and Chappell was meeting pop icon Elton John for pizza. But as her profile exploded, she began to feel as though some fans were encroaching on her private life. Chappell had drawn clear boundaries before: in January 2024, she told *NME* that she had stopped doing meet-and-greets before her gigs because these interactions were triggering her social anxiety. 'Sometimes I would have panic attacks after because I felt so overwhelmed,' she explained. She also implored fans not to call her by her government name, Kayleigh, because she wanted to keep her everyday self separate from her drag-influenced pop persona. In her *NME* interview she drew a parallel between herself and Trixie Mattel, a leading star of *RuPaul's Drag Race*: 'Can you imagine someone calling Trixie Mattel "Brian" when she's in drag?' Chappell noted pointedly.

By August 2024, the groundswell of unwanted attention had become too much for Chappell to bear. In an Instagram post, she lamented the fact she had been subjected to 'too many non-consensual physical and social interactions' since she became famous. 'I chose this career path because I love music and art and honouring my inner child,' she wrote. 'I do not accept harassment of any kind because I chose this path, nor do I deserve it.' Meanwhile, in a pair of straight-talking TikTok videos, she called out fans whose behaviour, she felt, had become increasingly 'creepy' and 'entitled'. Chappell had previously revealed on an episode of *The Comment Section* podcast that fans had found her sister's workplace and her parents' home address – intrusions that understandably rattled her. She also mentioned that some fans had started to follow her on the street, an unsettling state of affairs she mentioned again in her TikTok videos. 'If you saw a random woman on the street, would you yell at her from your car window?' Chappell asked rhetorically. 'Would you harass her in public? Would you go up to a random lady and say, "Can I take a photo with you?" ' Chappell also pondered whether fans would 'get mad' at a 'random lady' – as opposed to a famous pop star – who said no to a selfie request.

Chappell's comments sent shockwaves through the music industry and made fans of every stripe question their relationships with the artists they idolize. Pop fame has often been framed as a Faustian pact in which the artist accepts a certain loss of privacy in return for success, wealth and the affirming attention of their fans. But Chappell, always more outspoken and forward-thinking than the average performer, had decided it was time to rewrite the rules of engagement. Her rejection of fame's toxic flipside struck a chord with many because it crystallized a cultural shift that was already beginning to bubble. In an era where we're increasingly aware of the way global fame can corrode a performer's mental health, should we blindly assume that anyone 'owes' us a selfie, an Instagram interaction or a hug at the stage door? As Chappell noted on TikTok, 'It's weird how people think that you know a person just because you see them online or you listen to the art they make.'

Chappell's impassioned clap-back was met with concern and compassion from fellow performers. At a fan Q&A session ahead of her gig in Dublin on 17 September 2024, Chappell revealed that fellow pop alchemist Charli XCX was 'the first girl to reach out and check on me'. Given that Charli's profile also exploded during the middle months of 2024, when her sixth album, *Brat*, spawned a cultural moment dubbed 'Brat summer', it was powerful to picture her and Chappell standing shoulder to shoulder. In the past, female artists have often been pitted against one another by industry gatekeepers and media outlets – the supposed feud between Katy Perry and Taylor Swift that dominated gossip sites in 2014 is one particularly egregious example. But at a difficult and potentially pivotal moment in her career, Chappell was really benefiting from the support of her female peers.

In an interview with *The Face* magazine, in which she likened fame to an 'abusive ex-husband', Chappell revealed that she reached out to Lorde during a traumatizing incident at an airport. After she declined to sign posters for two men who didn't look like bona fide fans, Chappell was yelled at and followed into the passport control queue. While crying in the terminal's bathroom, Chappell messaged Lorde, who responded with a 'list of things' that Chappell should do to mitigate a similar situation. Chappell noted empathetically that Lorde, who released her 2013 breakthrough single 'Royals' as a 16-year-old, was 'just a baby' when she first had to deal with blindsiding global fame. In various other interviews, Chappell revealed that she has also received sympathetic messages from Katy Perry, Lady Gaga and another female artist who broke through spectacularly in 2024, Sabrina Carpenter. Chappell told *Rolling Stone* that she shares a particular bond with Sabrina because 'she just feels like everything is flying, and she's just barely hanging on.' Chappell could just as easily have been talking about herself.

Chappell poses with fellow Gen Z pop queens Sabrina Carpenter and Billie Eilish at the 2025 Grammy Awards.

Could Chappell's comments spark a significant shift in the relationship between artists and fans? On her BBC Sounds podcast *Miss Me?*, singer and actress Lily Allen said she considers it 'really amazing that [Chappell] knows herself and knows her boundaries and is happy to articulate that' in an uncompromising way. Lily became famous in the mid-2000s when social media was in its infancy – at the time, platforms such as MySpace gave savvy young artists an opportunity to build a fanbase and industry buzz without even having to leave home. But back then, no one realized that social media would also foster a greater sense of expectation from fans who felt 'closer' to their idols than ever before. By 2024, fans no longer had to wait at the stage door to interact with artists – they could just message them on Instagram or Twitter, as X was known until 2023. This illusion of accessibility had led to some fanbases becoming hyper-critical and even toxic. In June 2024, after her latest single, 'Lucky', was received less than rapturously, singer Halsey wrote in a Tumblr post that 'my own fans are hands down meaner to me than any other people on the planet'. Hopefully, Chappell's clear delineation of boundaries will have nipped this kind of situation in the bud.

But in the meantime, Chappell's relationship with her fame remains an ongoing negotiation. At the MTV Video Music Awards in September 2024, she clapped back at a photographer who told her to 'shut up' as she walked down the red carpet. As we mentioned earlier in the book – and legions of fans discussed online at the time – a distressed Chappell can be heard saying: 'You shut the fuck up. No, not me, bitch.' Asked about the incident later that evening, Chappell told *Entertainment Tonight* that

> *'for someone who gets* ***a lot of anxiety*** *around* ***people yelling*** *at you, the carpet is* ***horrifying****'.*

The following month, at the LA premiere of Olivia Rodrigo's Netflix concert film *GUTS*, Chappell appeared to confront the same photographer. In a clip that also went viral, she can be heard telling the snapper: 'You were so rude to me, and I deserve an apology for that.'

No Chappell fan wants to see her making headlines for berating a photographer, but these altercations highlight just how difficult she finds the flipside of fame. In a way, they also underline the core authenticity that makes Chappell stand out from the crowd. Her music is incredibly compelling because she doesn't self-censor or shy away from sharing messy truths. On 'Good Luck, Babe!', she warns a lover who is trying to deny her queerness that she'll end up pining for Chappell in the future. 'You're standing face to face with "I told you so",' she sings on the chorus. In the same vein, Chappell refuses to gloss over the negative aspects of her success: the unwanted attention, intrusions into her family life and allegedly disrespectful photographers.

So, maybe one takeaway is this: if we can't handle Chappell at her most scrappy and fractious, we don't truly deserve her when she's dazzling us on stage. Only by finding a way to navigate fame and fans' expectations on her own terms will Chappell be able to thrive. No one makes their best art when they're feeling like a cornered animal.

Chappell walks the red carpet at the MTV VMAS, an experience she described as 'horrifying', because it triggered her social anxiety.

A BONAFIDE SUPER NOVA

Chappell's Impact on Pop Culture

As Chappell's profile has grown, so has her platform, but this comes with a certain sense of expectation.

Modern pop stars are increasingly comfortable with using their voices for good, whether that's advocating for social change or simply encouraging their fan bases to vote. So, as Chappell's career progresses, she faces a tricky decision: does she get political or not? Some legends spend decades walking a delicate line to avoid offending any single demographic – Dolly Parton is the master at this. Others, like Madonna, are more willing to wade into controversial waters. So far, Chappell seems happy to speak out whenever her heart and conscience dictate. In a January 2025 interview with BBC Radio 1, she said self-deprecatingly: 'I think, actually, I'd be more successful if I was OK wearing a muzzle.' But whichever path she chooses, her very existence is already sparking important conversations about LGBTQIA+ issues in particular. To put it simply, Chappell matters.

POLITICAL INFLUENCER

In August 2024, Chappell broke out of the music news cycle and made political headlines for the first time. When the Democratic Party's presidential nominee Kamala Harris and her prospective VP Tim Walz dropped a new merch line, one item stood out: a camo-print baseball cap emblazoned with 'Harris Walz' in orange capital letters. Pop connoisseurs immediately spotted its resemblance to the Midwest Princess camo cap that Chappell was already selling through her online store. Soon after, Chappell drew attention to the similarity when she reposted photos of the two hats side by side with the comment 'is this real'.

It wasn't just real, but also a shrewd move from the Harris campaign, which had already used Chappell's female empowerment anthem 'Femininomenon' in a TikTok video. Mitch Cahn of Unionwear, the company manufacturing the campaign's merch, told *Women's Wear Daily* that they had sold 25,000 of the $40 caps in just 24 hours. 'We've been in business for 32 years. We never had an instance where we made a sample in the morning, and then they had sold a million dollar's worth of hats by the next morning,' he said.

In the process, the Harris–Walz campaign attracted a swell of positive press by aligning itself with the hottest new star on the planet. It was a particularly good look for Walz, a self-proclaimed 'Midwest dad' whose kids, 18 and 23, could feasibly be Chappell fans. It was also another milestone moment for the Midwest Princess herself. Less than four months after 'Good Luck, Babe!' had become her first Billboard Hot 100 hit, she was being used as leverage in a presidential election.

Of course, it also paved the way for Chappell to endorse Harris publicly: a big decision for anyone with a public profile, but especially for Chappell, who was still grappling with the heady expectations that came with her newfound fame. In an interview with the *Guardian* published in late September, Chappell insisted she didn't 'feel pressured to endorse' anyone. Without mentioning Harris or her Republican rival Donald Trump by name, she said: 'There's problems on both sides. I encourage people to use your critical thinking skills, use your vote – vote small, vote for what's going on in your city.'

Sadly, these measured comments didn't quell a small but noisy backlash from fans who felt she was sitting on the fence. Some trolls even floated the highly unlikely idea that Chappell might be a secret Trump supporter. A few days later, she clarified her stance in a pair of TikTok posts. Though she confirmed her intention to vote for Harris, Chappell reiterated the fact that she would not be endorsing either candidate because 'there is no way I can stand behind some of the left's completely transphobic and completely genocidal views'. She added firmly:

> *'I'm **not gonna settle** for what the options are that are in front of me, and you are **not gonna make me** feel bad for that.'*

Chappell had weathered her first political storm – one she didn't ask for and probably never saw coming. But by this point in her career, she was already well established as an agent of social change.

QUEER ICON

As 'Good Luck, Babe!', 'Pink Pony Club' and 'Hot to Go!' climbed the charts worldwide, media outlets including PinkNews and *K. Magazine* hailed Chappell as a 'queer icon' and a 'lesbian icon'. There's little doubt that she understands the power of these terms. In numerous interviews, she has spoken candidly and movingly about her ongoing journey to accept her sexuality. Speaking to *NME* in January 2024, Chappell confided that she sometimes feels 'not queer enough' because she hasn't only had relationships with women. 'It's kind of an imposter syndrome – that because I've dated men in the past, it doesn't make me as queer as someone who has only dated queer people,' she explained.

This imposter syndrome seems to be dissipating. At a concert in Cleveland, Ohio, in May 2024, Chappell confirmed that she now identifies as a lesbian. Sexuality is a spectrum, and Chappell is continuing to refine how she perceives and presents hers. In an interview with *Rolling Stone* published a few months later, she spoke about taking a less vocal approach to being out and proud.

> *'It's like, look,* ***I love being gay.*** *I just don't want to talk about it every second of every day,'*

she said. These comments will have resonated deeply with queer fans whose relationship with their own sexuality is also evolving. It takes time to progress from denial to acceptance, and then to find an inner peace with your queerness that doesn't necessarily involve shouting it from the rooftops.

CONVERSATION STARTER

Chappell is part of a vanguard of Gen Z and millennial artists enriching pop culture with unapologetic, authentic and often sexually charged queerness. Back in 2008, it was considered provocative when Katy Perry sang 'I kissed a girl and I liked it', but this song has since been criticized for framing same-sex attraction through the male gaze. On 'I Kissed a Girl', Perry almost seemed to be apologizing for her bicurious moment when she sang 'I hope my boyfriend don't mind it'. Now, Chappell and peers including Billie Eilish, Kehlani, Hayley Kiyoko, Renée Rapp and Romy are writing songs that put queer female sexuality front and centre. Eilish's hit 'Lunch' pivots on the risqué lyric 'I could eat that girl for lunch', while Chappell's 'Good Luck, Babe!' explores the messiness of dating someone who is trying to deny who they really are.

When Chappell sings 'you can kiss a hundred boys in bars, shoot another shot, try to stop the feeling', she is calling out the futility of this woman's attempts to suppress her own queerness. On the song's bridge, Chappell imagines this woman in the future, pining for her while stuck in an unsatisfying marriage with a man. The chorus payoff – 'You'd have to stop the world just to stop the feeling' – is simple but stunningly effective. Whether you believe a person's sexuality is rooted in nature, nurture or a combination of both, it's something that cannot be changed by mere force of will. Chappell has captured this eloquently in just 11 words.

Catchy, evocative and richly emotional, 'Good Luck, Babe!' is probably the first major pop song to explore the idea of compulsory heterosexuality, which theorizes that heterosexuality is enforced on people by a society that sees being straight as the default setting. Chappell has never discussed this idea in interviews, but she did tell *Rolling Stone* that 'Good Luck, Babe!' was her attempt to write a 'big anthemic pop song'. There's no doubt she succeeded: the result really shows off her gift for expressing poignant and profound feelings in a way that feels excitingly fresh. It duly became one of 2024's defining songs, peaking at number four in the US and being named the eighth biggest hit of the year by the UK's Official Charts Company.

With pencil-thin brows and statement eyeshadow, Chappell pays homage to legendary drag queen Divine at the 2024 Kentucky Pride Festival.

DRAG CHAMPION AND TRANS ALLY

'Good Luck, Babe!' is Chappell's most powerful queer rights anthem to date, but her music and artistry are also pushing pop culture forward in other ways. While other singers cast drag performers in their music videos, Chappell goes one step further by making drag a key facet of her identity. 'I feel like another girl in the local drag competition. Like another girl on *Drag Race*. I don't think I'm a judge yet,' she told *NME* in 2024. In the process, she is adding to the growing popularity of this once-marginalized art form, which has become increasingly mainstream over the last decade thanks to the global popularity of *RuPaul's Drag Race*. Even more significantly, Chappell has helped to clarify the idea that a cisgender woman can be a drag queen, something sexist drag gatekeepers have tried to deny in the past.

Chappell has also said she considers it her 'duty' to fight for transgender rights. During 2024's US presidential election, she told the *Guardian* that the change she most wants to see is 'trans rights' because 'they cannot have cis people making decisions for trans people, period'. She doubled down on this at the Grammy Awards in February 2025, when she told LGBTQ advocacy group GLAAD: 'They will never, no matter what happens, take trans joy away, and that has to be protected more than anything because I would not be here without trans girls. So just know that pop music is thinking about you and cares about you and I'm trying my best to stand up for you in every way that I can.'

Trans
Rights!

TEXAS

THE FUTURE

Chappell's career to date has followed a pretty unprecedented arc. As previous chapters of this book have explored, she's essentially an overnight success story a decade in the making. Will she inch back from the spotlight in the coming years, or will she continue to storm the charts and make headlines whenever she speaks out? Either way, there's no doubt that Chappell has already made a seismic impact on pop culture. By writing unstoppable pop anthems from an unapologetically queer perspective, she has become one of the defining artists of our time. At this point, the world truly is her oyster, so it's going to be fascinating to see how she shucks it from now on.

SONG CREDITS

Welcome to the Pink Pony Club

After Midnight
Written by Kayleigh Amstutz, Daniel Nigro and Casey Smith
2023 / Amusement / Island

Naked in Manhattan
Written by Kayleigh Amstutz, Daniel Nigro and Skyler Stonestreet
Written by Kayleigh Amstutz and Daniel Nigro
2022 / Amusement / Island

Die Young
Written by Kayleigh Amstutz and Andrew Wells
2017 / Atlantic

California
Written by Kayleigh Amstutz and Daniel Nigro
2020 / Atlantic / Amusement / Island

The Origin Story of a Midwest Princess

Good Hurt
Written by Kayleigh Amstutz, Jennifer Decilveo, Edvard Erfjord, Henrik Michelsen and Andrew Wells
2017 / Atlantic

Sugar High
Written by Kayleigh Amstutz and Phili Stelios
2017 / Atlantic

Bad for You
Written by Kayleigh Amstutz, Jennifer Decilveo and Andrew Wells
2017 / Atlantic

Bitter
Written by Kayleigh Amstutz
Atlantic / 2017

Naked in Manhattan
Written by Kayleigh Amstutz, Daniel Nigro and Skyler Stonestreet
2022 / Amusement / Island

My Kink Is Karma
Written by Kayleigh Amstutz, Daniel Nigro and Justin Tranter
2022 / Amusement / Island

Femininomenon
Written by Kayleigh Amstutz and Daniel Nigro
2022 / Amusement / Island

Casual
Written by Kayleigh Amstutz, Daniel Nigro and Morgan St. Jean
2022 / Amusement / Island

A Not-so-casual Start

Super Graphic Ultra Modern Girl
Written by Kayleigh Amstutz, Annika Bennett, Daniel Nigro, Jonah Shy and Mike Wise
2023 / Amusement / Island

After Midnight
Written by Kayleigh Amstutz, Daniel Nigro and Casey Smith
2023 / Amusement / Island

Picture You
Written by Kayleigh Amstutz and Daniel Nigro
2023 / Amusement / Island

Coffee
Written by Kayleigh Amstutz, Maya Kurchner, Eric Leva and Daniel Nigro
2023 / Amusement / Island

The Giver
Written by Kayleigh Amstutz and Daniel Nigro
2025 / Amusement / Island

The Rise & Rise of a Femininomenon

Good Luck, Babe!
Written by Kayleigh Amstutz, Daniel Nigro and Justin Tranter
2024 / Amusement / Island

Super Iconic Ultra Famous Girl

'Pink Pony Club'
Written by Kayleigh Amstutz and Daniel Nigro
2020 / Atlantic / Amusement / Island

Naked in Manhattan
Written by Kayleigh Amstutz, Daniel Nigro and Skyler Stonestreet
2022 / Amusement / Island

After Midnight
Written by Kayleigh Amstutz, Daniel Nigro and Casey Smith
2023 / Amusement / Island

The Giver
Written by Kayleigh Amstutz and Daniel Nigro
2025 / Amusement / Island

Red Wine Supernova
Written by Kayleigh Amstutz, Lisa Hickox, Amy Kuney, Daniel Nigro and Annie Schindel
2023 / Amusement / Island

Good Luck, Babe!
Written by Kayleigh Amstutz, Daniel Nigro and Justin Tranter
2024 / Amusement / Island

A Bonafide Supernova

I Kissed a Girl
Written by Katy Perry, Lukasz Gottwald, Max Martin and Cathy Dennis
2008 / Capitol

Lunch
Written by Billie Eilish O'Connell and Finneas O'Connell
2024 / Darkroom / Interscope

Good Luck, Babe!
Written by Kayleigh Amstutz, Daniel Nigro and Justin Tranter
2024 / Amusement / Island

REFERENCES

Welcome to the Pink Pony Club

Levine, Nick. Chappell Roan: the pop supernova who feels like one of the *Drag Race* girls – *NME*, 5 February 2024.

The Origin Story of a Midwest Princess

Levine, Nick. Chappell Roan: the pop supernova who feels like one of the *Drag Race* girls – *NME*, 5 February 2024.

D'Souza, Shaad. Chappell Roan, pop's next big thing: 'I grew up thinking being gay was a sin' – *Guardian*, 29 December 2023.

Holman, Gregory J. Chappell Roan is a singer from Willard. She just made the big time – *Springfield News-Leader*, 17 August 2017.

Spanos, Brittany. Chappell Roan Is the Independent 'Thrift Store Pop Star' Ready to Take Over the World – *Rolling Stone*, 27 October 2022.

Yohn, Madison. We Sat Down With Chappell Roan, A Springfield Native Turned Pop Artist – Visit Springfield, 17 February 2023.

Sherman, Maria. A conversation with Chappell Roan, the yodeling, queer pop icon of tomorrow – Associated Press, 3 October 2023.

Fromson, Audrey. Chappell Roan on Making Pop Music and Giving Back – *Vanity Fair*, 18 September 2023.

Levine, Nick. Chappell Roan is becoming the queer pop icon of her dreams – *NME*, 21 June 2023.

Shafer, Ellise. Confessions of a 'Midwest Princess': How Chappell Roan's Debut Album Arose From the 'Deep Pits of Hell' to Become a 'Dream Come True' – *Variety*, 22 September 2023.

Solomon, Kate. 'Fame is like going through puberty': Chappell Roan on sexuality, superstardom and the joy of drag – *Guardian*, 20 September 2024.

Exclusive Interview with 'Chappell Roan' – *Illustrate*, 19 June 2022.

Lindsay, Kathryn. The Drop: Exclusive Music Video Premiere For Chappell Roan's 'Die Young' – Refinery29, 3 January 2018.

Azzopardi, Chris. On the Tour Bus with Chappell Roan: Everything the Superstar Told Us About Drag, Making Straight Boys Dance and Being Part of Pop Music's 'Alliance of Queer Girlies' – PrideSource, 6 August 2024.

Ribner, Sonya. Slumber Party Pop: A New Authenticity with Chappell Roan – Cherwell, 12 August 2022.

A Not-so-casual Start

Liberty, Cami. Chappell Roan: Interview – Unclear, 10 December 2017.

Gustafson, Alice. Chappell Roan: how an unforgettable night at a gay club led to 'Pink Pony Club' – Headliner, date unknown.

Zyda, Rachel. A Chat with: Chappell Roan – *Anchr Magazine*, 2 April 2018.

Kato, Brooke. Chappell Roan to show off evolving sound at The Lost Horizon – The Daily Orange, 20 February 2018.

Bardsley, Miranda. Hitmakers: Dan Nigro on the making of Chappell Roan's global smash 'Good Luck, Babe!' – *Music Week*, 17 December 2024.

Wakeam, Kira; Chang, Ailsa; Intagliata, Christopher. How Chappell Roan's producer Dan Nigro crafts pop hits for a new generation – NPR, 23 December 2024.

Shafer, Ellise. Confessions of a 'Midwest Princess': How Chappell Roan's Debut Album Arose From the 'Deep Pits of Hell' to Become a 'Dream Come True' – *Variety*, 22 September 2023.

Levine, Nick. Chappell Roan: the pop supernova who feels like one of the *Drag Race* girls – *NME*, 5 February 2024.

Spanos, Brittany. Chappell Roan Is the Independent 'Thrift Store Pop Star' Ready to Take Over the World – *Rolling Stone*, 27 October 2022.

Levine, Nick. Chappell Roan is becoming the queer pop icon of her dreams – *NME*, 21 June 2023.

Orbison, Bonnie. Chappell Roan – 'Naked In Manhattan' – Bonnie's Legends, 25 February 2023.

Treadgold, Emily. Chappell Roan wants to create a 'Femininomenon' – Earmilk, 17 August 2022.

The Rise & Rise of a Femininomenon

Mier, Tomás. How Chappell Roan Found 'Complete Freedom and Euphoria' Making Her Debut Album – *Rolling Stone*, 21 September 2023.

Levine, Nick. Chappell Roan: the pop supernova who feels like one of the *Drag Race* girls – *NME*, 5 February 2024.

Wagmeister, Elizabeth. Chappell Roan may have had the biggest Lollapalooza set of all time – CNN, 5 August 2024.

Exposito, Suzy. Kesha Freed Herself. Now She's Saving Music – *Elle*, 3 October 2024.

Solomon, Kate. 'Fame is like going through puberty': Chappell Roan on sexuality, superstardom and the joy of drag – *Guardian*, 20 September 2024.

Spanos, Brittany. Why A 'Good Luck, Babe!' Video Probably Isn't Coming Soon – And More Things We Learned Hanging With Chappell Roan – *Rolling Stone*, 15 September 2024.

Spanos, Brittany. Chappell Roan Is a Pop Supernova. Nothing About It Has Been Easy – *Rolling Stone*, 10 September 2024.

Zyda, Rachel. A Chat with: Chappell Roan – *Anchr Magazine*, 2 April 2018.

Levine, Nick. Chappell Roan: the pop supernova who feels like one of the *Drag Race* girls – N*ME*, 5 February 2024.

Exposito, Suzy. Kesha Freed Herself. Now She's Saving Music – *Elle*, 3 October 2024.

McCarthy, Lauren. Chappell Roan Steals The Show – *Nylon*, 4 April 2024.

Cai, Delia. The femininomenonal ascent of Chappell Roan – *The Face*, 16 September 2024.

Exclusive Interview with 'Chappell Roan' – *Illustrate*, 19 June 2022.

Martoccio, Angie. Stevie Nicks: 'I Believe in the Church of Stevie' – *Rolling Stone*, 24 October 2024.

Your Favourite Artist's Favourite Artists

Richards, Megan. Chappell Roan Talks Boston Show, Debut Album and More – Five Cent Sound, 3 November 2023.

Wally, Maxine. Alanis Morissette Aims To Be a Lifeline for Young Female Artists – *W*, 10 August 2024.

Atkinson, Kate. Interview with Chappell Roan – I Dream of Vinyl, 7 May 2020.

Dailey, Hannah. Chappell Roan Praises Ariana Grande's *Eternal Sunshine*, Reveals She's 'So Excited' for *Wicked* – *Billboard*, 29 August 2024.

Yang, Bowen. Chappell Roan and Bowen Yang on Queers, Fears and Surviving Superstardom – *Interview*, 19 August 2024.

Zyda, Rachel. A Chat with: Chappell Roan – *Anchr Magazine*, 2 April 2018.

Fowlkes, Tamia. 'Midwest Princess' Chappell Roan talks queerness, girlhood and growing up – *Milwaukee Sentinel Journal*, 4 October 2023.

Shafer, Ellise. Confessions of a 'Midwest Princess': How Chappell Roan's Debut Album Arose From the 'Deep Pits of Hell' to Become a 'Dream Come True' – *Variety*, 22 September 2023.

Luscombe, Belinda. 2024 Icon of the Year: Elton John – 11 December 2024.

A Kaleidoscope of Inspiration

Levine, Nick. Chappell Roan: the pop supernova who feels like one of the *Drag Race* girls – *NME*, 5 February 2024.

Summers, Joan. Chappell Roan Is Taking It – Paper, 4 June 2024.

Gustafson, Alice. Chappell Roan: how an unforgettable night at a gay club led to 'Pink Pony Club' – Headliner, date unknown.

Sessoms, Janelle. Chappell Roan is Leading a 'Maximalism Moment' in Beauty, According to Her Makeup Artist – *Fashionista*, 5 June 2024.

Levine, Nick. Chappell Roan is becoming the queer pop icon of her dreams – *NME*, 21 June 2023.

Stock, Michaela. Chappell Roan: Red-Haired Supernova – *Revue*, 31 May 2024.

Orbison, Bonnie. Chappell Roan – 'Naked In Manhattan' – Bonnie's Legends, 25 February 2023.

Sillitti, Par Flavio. *Je suis allée dans un club gay et ça a changé ma vie: Chappell Roan est la pop star dont le monde a besoin* – Konbini, 7 June 2024.

Chappell Roan: The Struggle of Not Feeling 'Gay Enough' – @capitalbuzz on TikTok, 10 June 2024.

Spanos, Brittany. Chappell Roan Is a Pop Supernova. Nothing About It Has Been Easy – *Rolling Stone*, 10 September 2024.

My Kink Is Chappell

Spanos, Brittany. Chappell Roan Is a Pop Supernova. Nothing About It Has Been Easy – *Rolling Stone*, 10 September 2024.

Factora, James. Chappell Roan on Falling in Love With Makeup and Finding Peace Amid Fame – Them, 5 February 2025.

Wolper, Caitlin. 'How Can We Make It Campier?' Dressing rising pop star Chappell Roan is about making the impossible happen without getting in trouble – *Vulture*, 24 May 2024.

Holtermann, Callie. How Chappell Roan's Stylist Turned Her Into a Creepy Swan (Twice) – *The New York Times*, 25 June 2024.

Ribeiro, Julian. Creative Director Genesis Webb Takes Us Inside Chappell Roan's VMA Takeover – *Interview*, 14 September 2024.

Super Iconic Ultra Famous Girl

Levine, Nick. Chappell Roan: the pop supernova who feels like one of the *Drag Race* girls – *NME*, 5 February 2024.

Spanos, Brittany. Chappell Roan Is a Pop Supernova. Nothing About It Has Been Easy – *Rolling Stone*, 10 September 2024.

A Bonafide Supernova

Botelho, Renan. Kamala Harris and Tim Walz Sell 'Million Dollars' Worth of Hats' in Less Than 24 Hours With Viral Chappell Roan-inspired Camo Merch – *Women's Wear Daily*, 8 August 2024.

Solomon, Kate. 'Fame is like going through puberty': Chappell Roan on sexuality, superstardom and the joy of drag – *Guardian*, 20 September 2024.

Levine, Nick. Chappell Roan: the pop supernova who feels like one of the *Drag Race* girls – *NME*, 5 February 2024.

Spanos, Brittany. Chappell Roan Is a Pop Supernova. Nothing About It Has Been Easy – *Rolling Stone*, 10 September 2024.

Bloom, Allison. WATCH: Grammys Best New Artist Chappell Roan Shares Message of Resilience with GLAAD on the red carpet 'They will never, no matter what happens, take trans joy away.' – GLAAD, 3 February 2025.

PICTURE CREDITS

Abhijeet Gourav/Unsplash: 127; Adam Gritco/Unsplash: 128; Alexander Grey/Unsplash: 126, 130, 132; Alina Rubo/Unsplash: 130; AllUneed/Shutterstock: 127; Amir Seilsepour/Unsplash: 131; Anastasiia Ornarin/Unsplash: 126; Angus Gray/Unsplash : 126; Annette Batista/Unsplash: 126; Associated Press/Alamy Stock Photo: 42, 45, 51, 53, 54–55, 62, 63, 64, 81, 86, 94, 123, 124, 129, 136, 141, 149, 153, 154–155; Astrida Valigorsky/Getty Images: 17, 125, 131, 146; Ben Iwara/Unsplash: 128; bombermoon/Shutterstock: 130; Brice Cooper/Unsplash: 132; cassp/iStock: 129; CBS Photo Archive/Getty Images: 111; ChameleonsEye/Shutterstock: 133; Christopher; Polk/Getty Images: 41; Dania Maxwell/Getty Images: 113; Dekler Ph/Unsplash: 130; Denis OREA/Shutterstock: 129; DFree/Shutterstock: 131; Dylan Hunter/Unsplash: 130; Emmanuel Boldo/Unsplash: 131; Everett Collection Inc/Alamy Stock Photo: 72; EXImages/Alamy Stock Photo: 68; Francis Specker/Alamy Stock Photo: 67; Fredrik Solli Wandem/Unsplash: 132; Gabrielle Henderson/Unsplash: 133; Gian D/Unsplash: 133; Imagespace/Alamy Stock Photo: 75; Jacqueline Brandwayn/Unsplash: 130; Jamie Street/Unsplash: 130, 133; Jared Subia/Unsplash: 129; Jason Leung/Unsplash: 132; Jim Bennett/Getty Images: 12; Joe Fallico/Shutterstock: 132; John Shearer/Getty Images: 83; Joni Ludlow/Unsplash: 127; Karsten Winegeart/Unsplash: 132; Katja Ogrin/Getty Images: 97; Katy Blackwood/Alamy Stock Photo: 85; Kenny Eliason/Unsplash: 129; Kevin Mazur/Getty Images: 139; Kiselev Andrey Valerevich/Shutterstock: 131; LANDMARK MEDIA/Alamy Stock Photo: 66; Lital Levy/Unsplash: 129; Lukasz Rawa/Unsplash: 126; Maarten de Boer/Getty Images: 69; Marleen Moise/Getty Images: 99; MediaPunch Inc/Alamy Stock Photo: 70, 71; Meina Yin/Unsplash: 133; MICHAEL TRAN/AFP/Getty Images: 30; Mila Vasileva/Unsplash: 131; Misael Nevarez/Unsplash: 128; Montylov/Unsplash: 131; Morten Andreassen/Unsplash: 128; Nana Fuzimi/Unsplash: 133; Natasha Moustache/Getty Images: 10[illegible]; NBC/Getty Images: 104, 117; Néstor J. Beremblum/Alamy Stock Photo: 77; Newscom/Alamy Stock Photo: 58, 65, 81, 109; Nina Westervelt/Getty Images: 115; No Revisions/Unsplash: 133; PA Images/Alamy Stock Photo: 79; Patti McConville/Alamy Stock Photo: 38; Pavel Aliakseyeu/Shutterstock: 128; Pawel Szymanski/Unsplash: 132; Pictorial Press Ltd/Alamy Stock Photo: 58, 66, 60, 73, 89; PictureLux/The Hollywood Archive/Alamy Stock Photo: 80; Rodolfo Sassano/Alamy Stock Photo: 61; Rodolfo Sassano/Alamy Stock Photo: 76; SaltedLife/Shutterstock: 127; Seprimor/Shutterstock: 13[illegible]; Sipa US/Alamy Stock Photo: 107; Stephen J. Cohen/Getty Images: 93, [illegible]50; Steve Collender/Shutterstock: 129; surachet khamsuk/Shutterstock: 133; Sven Kucinic/Unsplash: 128; Szabo Viktor/Unsplash: 126; Ted Somerville/Alamy Stock Photo: 46, 47, 119; The Washington Post/Getty Images: 4, 15, 28, 33, 35, 125, 132, 133; Tim Mossholder/Unsplash: 132; UPI/Alamy Stock Photo: 49, 121, 153; Vincent Anderson/Unsplash: 126; Vittorio Zunino Celotto/Getty Images: 144; Vivien Killilea/Getty Images: 20, 24; WENN Rights Ltd/Alamy Stock Photo: 74, 78; WWD/Getty Images: 124, 127; Yesina Kseniya/Shutterstock: 127; Zeke Tucker/Unsplash: 127; ZUMA Press, Inc./Alamy Stock Photo: 7, 90.

First published in Great Britain in 2025
by Greenfinch

An imprint of Quercus Editions Limited
Carmelite House
50 Victoria Embankment
London EC4Y 0DZ

An Hachette UK company

The authorized representative in the EEA is Hachette Ireland, 8 Castlecourt Centre, Dublin 15, D15 XTP3, Ireland (email: info@hbgi.ie)

A CIP catalogue record for this book is available from the British Library

HB ISBN 978-1-52944-712-5

10 9 8 7 6 5 4 3 2 1

Designed by Beth Free, Studio Nic + Lou

Printed and bound in Italy by L.E.G.O. S.p.A.

Papers used by Greenfinch are from well-managed forests and other responsible sources.

THANK YOU

Thank you to Emily Arbis for commissioning me to write this book and shepherding me so smoothly through the editing process. The deadline was quite tight but you made sure that it never felt fraught or frantic, which made all the difference. Thank you also to Lucy Kingett, who gave consistently great notes and punched up each chapter to make it as sharp as possible. It was honestly a pleasure to work with both of you.

Thank you to CJ Banks, Inga Rock and Tequila Thirst: the talented drag performers who generously shared their experiences of working with Chappell. I really enjoyed speaking to all of you and hope to see you owning the stage soon.

Thank you to NME *for commissioning me to interview Chappell, not once but twice. Life as a freelance writer is pretty precarious, so I'm grateful – and kind of amazed – to be contributing regularly after 15 years.*

Thank you to Adam, David and Howell for creating a group chat where no pop culture reference is ever too niche or random. You never know when this stuff will prove useful (actually, I do – it's in my copy).

Thank you to Neil for offering great advice and putting up with having Chappell's album on display in our living room for the last nine months. Sorry king, but it's not going anywhere.

And, finally, thank you to my family for always being supportive and understanding that watching Popworld *on Sunday morning was an essential part of my education. I'm genuinely so grateful to have parents who text me whenever Vernon Kay plays 'Pink Pony Club'.*

Nick Levine is a freelance journalist who specializes in music, culture and LGBTQ issues. He contributes regularly to publications including *NME*, *BBC Culture*, *Time Out London*, *The i*, *GAY TIMES*, *Attitude AnOther* and *The Big Issue*. This year he has interviewed musicians including Chappell Roan, Shawn Mendes and Nelly Furtado, as well as other eminent figures including Jodie Foster and Alan Hollinghurst. In previous years, he has interviewed Britney Spears, Ariana Grande, Miley Cyrus, Lady Gaga and many more. He is a member of the BRITS voting academy and a fellow of the RSA.

CHAPPELL

ROAN

CHAPPELL

ROAN

CHAPPELL